ABOUT THE EDITOR

Simon Van Booy is the author of *The Secret Lives of People in Love* and *Love Begins in Winter*, which in 2009 won the Frank O'Connor International Short Story Award. He has written for *The New York Times*, *The Daily Telegraph*, *The Times*, *The Guardian*, and NPR. He lives in New York City where he lectures at the School of Visual Arts and is involved in the Rutgers Early College Humanities program for young adults living in underserved communities. His work has been translated into nine different languages.

WHY WE FIGHT

ALSO BY SIMON VAN BOOY

FICTION

Love Begins in Winter

The Secret Lives of People in Love

NONFICTION

Why We Need Love (editor)

Why Our Decisions Don't Matter (editor)

WHY WE FIGHT

Edited by Simon Van Booy

HARPER**PERENNIAL** MODERN**THOUGHT**

NEW YORK • LONDON • TORONTO • SYDNEY • NEW DELHI • AUCKLAND

HARPER**PERENNIAL** ✹ MODERN**THOUGHT**

HarperCollins books may be purchased for educational, business, or
sales promotional use. For information, please write: Special Markets
Department, HarperCollins Publishers, 10 East 53rd Street, New
York, NY 10022.

FIRST EDITION

Designed by Justin Dodd

Library of Congress Cataloging-in-Publication data is available upon
request.

ISBN 978-0-06-184556-7

10 11 12 13 14 OV/RRD 10 9 8 7 6 5 4 3 2 1

Dedicated to my brother, Darren,
with whom I bravely fought
in the battle of the bunk beds

CONTENTS

PREFACE TO THE SERIES

My hope for these books is to present interesting and exciting philosophical ideas in a straightforward, but intelligent, language that can be understood by everyone. I believe that philosophy is a subject we have a natural gift for, but a subject often regarded as one with no practical value—and closed to anyone outside the walls of universities. I am committed to the idea that these central questions of life are part of our everyday lives—that we all possess the skill and agility to tackle them, and that by pondering them, we can experience more fulfillment in our relationships, in our work, and in how we view ourselves.

Inside these books are readings, poems, quotations, and visual images that will inspire you to continue exploring the subject for years to come. I have tried my best to present philosophical ideas with no immediate resolution as immediately accessible for everyday thinking.

These volumes are not meant to convince you of anything, to be a definitive source, or to offer any new insights on a topic. Their purpose is simply to introduce you to an age-old theme that quite possibly has already taken a key role in your life.

To begin then, let me tell you about a small statue I once saw in a New Orleans public park. The young man of marble who stood before me (discolored by years of affection from birds) was holding a book to his heart with one hand, while using his other hand to pick a grape from a vine.

If the grape were to represent life, and the book over his heart, knowledge, then one interpretation may be that book learning and actual life experience complement each other. So by reading about other people's experiences in this book, we may begin to understand ourselves with fresh insight. Reading reassures us that no matter how alone we might feel, there are many others—spread as wide as history itself—who have felt the same way we have, who have occupied the rooms we find ourselves locked in at various points of our lives.

One celebrated aspect of literature is that unlike the ambitious exactitude of science, literature is often ambiguous—meaning that two people might have very different ideas about what a play, poem, or book is about. While at first this implied vagueness might seem detrimental to literature, it's one of its sustaining virtues, and allows people from different cultures, and even different time periods, to learn something about their own lives from a single story. If a story were viewed as a literal history, one could argue that it wouldn't be quite as useful—because history can easily be disproved, whereas story and myth are more like advice whispered to us by a wise grandmother. Many of the great geniuses who lived over the last five thousand years were not writers at all, but oral storytellers who left it up to others to write down what they said.

Stories, parables, and dialogues were their preferred method of teaching—in other words, instead of saying to a lazy child: "Go tidy your room now!" our greatest thinkers would probably have begun with something like: "There was once a girl who never tidied her room . . ."

INTRODUCTION

Many people have had the experience of lying awake at night going over the details of a recent argument or conflict, while others are burdened with the memory of a war or a violent event. Some people were bullied at school, while others did the bullying.

Humans have been fighting with one another, with their environment, and with themselves for thousands of years. But why do people fight? Is fighting something we are born to do, or is it something we learn? Are some environments more likely to induce fighting than others?

This book is an introduction to how fighting has been addressed in different contexts throughout the ages, so that as readers, we might gain a greater understanding of why we do it—why we fight.

WHY WE FIGHT

The story of Cain and Abel is one of the most well-known ancient stories. This story has been interpreted in many different ways throughout the ages, not only in literature, but also in painting. For modern scholars of the Bible, Cain and Abel is an etiological story that explores the nature of an aggressive biblical tribe called the Kenites. However, for most people it's a story about murder, crime, punishment, envy, and sibling rivalry—all major themes in ancient literature.

In many ancient stories and myths, people fight because of excessive pride—an emotion that often arises after the experience of rejection.

At God's refusal to favor Cain, Cain's heart hardens at being rejected and he is unable to subdue his pride. Despite being warned by God about these feelings, Cain is not able to rise above the emotions that lead him to kill his brother.

Cain slays his brother and then is forced to spend the remainder of his life coping with the consequences. So in a way, a part of Cain himself is slain the moment his brother dies. This story allows the reader to empathize with the urge to kill someone as a human feeling while at the same time presenting the social and psychological consequences of something that can so easily be done.

from *Genesis IV*

And the human knew Eve his woman and she conceived and bore Cain, and she said. "I have got me a man with the LORD." And she bore as well his brother, Abel, and Abel became a herder of sheep while Cain was a tiller of the soil. And it happened in the course of time that Cain brought from the fruit of the soil an offering to the LORD. And Abel too had brought from the choice firstlings of his flock, and the LORD regarded Abel and his offering but He did not regard Cain and his offering, and Cain was very incensed, and his face fell. And the LORD said to Cain.

> Why are you incensed,
> and why is your face fallen?
> For whether you offer well,
> or whether you do not,
> at the tent flap sin crouches
> and for you is its longing
> but you will rule over it.

And Cain said to Abel his brother, "Let us go out to the field." And when they were in the field. Cain rose against Abel his brother and killed him. And the LORD said to Cain. "Where is Abel your brother?" And he said. "I do not know. Am I my brother's keeper?" And He said. "What have you done? Listen! your brother's blood cries out to me from the soil. And so, cursed shall you be by the soil that gaped with its mouth to take your brother's blood from your hand. If you till the soil, it will no longer give you its strength. A restless wanderer shall you be on the earth." And Cain said to the Lord, "My punishment is too great to bear. Now that You have driven me this day from the soil and I must hide from Your presence. I shall be a restless wanderer on the earth and whoever finds me will kill me." And the Lord said to him. "Therefore whoever kills Cain shall suffer sevenfold vengeance." And the Lord set a mark upon Cain so that whoever found him would not slay him.

James Tissot, *Cain Leadeth Abel to Death,* 1896–1902

It is easier to commit murder than to justify it.

—Aemilius Papinianus

Greek dramatist Sophocles was born in 496 BCE, died in 406 BCE, and was greatly admired in his own time, holding positions in the military, government, and religious institutions. Sophocles also acted in the theater, and was known for his musical skill and comedic dexterity with props. Although he wrote over one hundred plays, only a handful have survived.

Antigone is a short but intense play about a young woman who wants to bury her brother's corpse in a way that honors her religious beliefs. However, the new local leader, Creon (also Antigone's uncle), views Antigone's brother as a traitor to the state, and has forbidden his burial by anyone.

For most of the play, Creon and Antigone argue it out—neither willing to bend or compromise, both completely self-assured in their unwavering single-mindedness.

Sophocles

from *Antigone*

CREON

Speak, girl, with head bent low and downcast eyes,
Does thou plead guilty or deny the deed?

ANTIGONE

Guilty. I did it, I deny it not.

CREON (TO GUARD)

Sirrah, begone whither thou wilt, and thank
Thy luck that thou hast 'scaped a heavy charge.
(TO ANTIGONE)
Now answer this plain question, yes or no,
Wast thou acquainted with the interdict?

ANTIGONE

I knew, all knew; how should I fail to know?

CREON

And yet wert bold enough to break the law?

ANTIGONE

Yea, for these laws were not ordained of Zeus,

And she who sits enthroned with gods below,

Justice, enacted not these human laws.

Nor did I deem that thou, a mortal man,

Could'st by a breath annul and override

The immutable unwritten laws of Heaven.

They were not born today nor yesterday;

They die not; and none knoweth whence they sprang.

I was not like, who feared no mortal's frown,

To disobey these laws and so provoke

The wrath of Heaven. I knew that I must die,

E'en hadst thou not proclaimed it; and if death

Is thereby hastened, I shall count it gain.

For death is gain to him whose life, like mine,

Is full of misery. Thus my lot appears

Not sad, but blissful; for had I endured

To leave my mother's son unburied there,

I should have grieved with reason, but not now.

And if in this thou judgest me a fool,

Methinks the judge of folly's not acquit.

CHORUS

A stubborn daughter of a stubborn sire,

This ill-starred maiden kicks against the pricks.

CREON

Well, let her know the stubbornest of wills
Are soonest bended, as the hardest iron,
O'er-heated in the fire to brittleness,
Flies soonest into fragments, shivered through.
A snaffle curbs the fieriest steed, and he
Who in subjection lives must needs be meek.
But this proud girl, in insolence well-schooled,
First overstepped the established law, and then—
A second and worse act of insolence—
She boasts and glories in her wickedness.
Now if she thus can flout authority
Unpunished, I am woman, she the man.
But though she be my sister's child or nearer
Of kin than all who worship at my hearth,
Nor she nor yet her sister shall escape
The utmost penalty, for both I hold,
As arch-conspirators, of equal guilt.
Bring forth the older; even now I saw her
Within the palace, frenzied and distraught.
The workings of the mind discover oft
Dark deeds in darkness schemed, before the act.
More hateful still the miscreant who seeks
When caught, to make a virtue of a crime.

ANTIGONE

Would'st thou do more than slay thy prisoner?

CREON

Not I, thy life is mine, and that's enough.

ANTIGONE

Why dally then? To me no word of thine
Is pleasant: God forbid it e'er should please;
Nor am I more acceptable to thee.
And yet how otherwise had I achieved
A name so glorious as by burying
A brother? so my townsmen all would say,
Where they not gagged by terror, Manifold
A king's prerogatives, and not the least
That all his acts and all his words are law.

CREON

Of all these Thebans none so deems but thou.

ANTIGONE

These think as I, but bate their breath to thee.

CREON

Hast thou no shame to differ from all these?

ANTIGONE

To reverence kith and kin can bring no shame.

CREON

Was his dead foeman not thy kinsman too?

ANTIGONE

One mother bare them and the self-same sire.

CREON

Why cast a slur on one by honoring one?

ANTIGONE

The dead man will not bear thee out in this.

CREON

Surely, if good and evil fare alive.

ANTIGONE

The slain man was no villain but a brother.

CREON

The patriot perished by the outlaw's brand.

ANTIGONE

Nathless the realms below these rites require.

CREON

Not that the base should fare as do the brave.

ANTIGONE

Who knows if this world's crimes are virtues there?

CREON

Not even death can make a foe a friend.

ANTIGONE

My nature is for mutual love, not hate.

CREON

Die then, and love the dead if thou must;
No woman shall be the master while I live.

You shall not treat the people with arrogance, nor shall you roam the earth proudly. GOD does not like the arrogant showoffs.

—*The Koran*

Pride goeth before destruction, and an haughty spirit before a fall.

—*Proverbs*

Thich Nhat Hanh is a Buddhist Zen master, poet, and human rights activist. Born in 1926, he has devoted his life to helping individuals with their basic needs for survival and to find a sense of deep fulfillment through self-reflection, mindfulness, compassion, and nonviolence. Nhat Hanh publicly requested Dr. Martin Luther King Jr. to oppose the Vietnam War and was nominated for the Nobel Peace Prize one year later. In 1982, he founded Plum Village, a Buddhist community in France, where he continues his human rights advocacy and runs retreat programs.

In his book, *True Love*, Nhat Hanh tackles the issue of pride as a source of conflict in a relationship between a husband and wife.

Thich Nhat Hanh

from *True Love*

I would like to tell you a story from my country. A young man went off to war, leaving his pregnant wife behind. Two years later, he was able to return home, and the young woman went with their young son to meet her husband. They cried together out of joy. In Vietnam, in our tradition, when an event of this kind takes place, it has to be announced to the ancestors. So the young father asked his wife to go to the market to buy the things that are needed for the offering that is placed on the altar to the ancestors. Such an altar is found in every house. Each morning we burn a stick of incense to our ancestors on this altar, and in this way we make a connection with them. Burning this incense, adorning the altar with photographs of our ancestors, and dusting the shrine off are very important gestures. These are moments in which we come in contact with our ancestors. There are people living in the world who are completely uprooted because they do not practice such a turning toward their ancestors.

So the young wife went off to the market. During this time, the young father was trying to convince his child to call him Daddy. The little boy refused: "Mister, you're not my daddy. My daddy is somebody else. He visits us every night and my mommy talks to him every night, and very often she cries with him. And every time my mommy sits down, he sits down too. Every time she lies down, he lies down too." After he heard these words, the young father's happiness entirely evaporated. His heart turned into a block of ice. He felt hurt, deeply humiliated, and that is why, when his wife came home, he would no longer look at her or speak a word to her. He ignored her. The woman herself began to suffer: she felt humiliated, hurt. When the offering was placed on the altar, the young father burned the incense, recited the prayers to the ancestors, and did the four traditional prostrations. Then he picked the mat up instead of leaving it there for his wife so she could do the four prostrations in her turn. In his mind he thought that she was not qualified to present herself before the ancestors, and she was humiliated by this.

After the ceremony, he didn't stay at the house to eat but went to the village and spent the day in a bar. He tried to forget his suffering by drinking alcohol, and he did not come back to the house until very late at night. The following day, it was the same thing, and this went on for several days in a row. The young woman could not take it anymore. Her suffering was so great that in the end she threw herself in the river and drowned.

When the young father heard this news, he returned to the house, and that night he was the one who went to get the lamp and lit it. Suddenly the child cried out: "Mister, Mister, it's my daddy, he's come back!" And he pointed to the shadow of his father on the wall. "You know, Mister, my father comes every night. Mommy talks to him and sometimes she cries; and every time she sits down my daddy sits down too."

In reality, this woman had been alone in the house too much and every night she had talked to her shadow: "My dear one, you are so far away from me. How can I raise my child all by myself? . . . You must come back home soon." She would cry, and of course every time she sat down, the shadow would also sit down. Now the husband's false perception was no longer there, but it was too late—his wife was already dead.

A misperception is something that can destroy an entire family. The Buddha told us a number of times that we are subject to misperceptions in our everyday life. Therefore we have to pay close attention to our perceptions. There are people who hang on to their misperceptions for ten or twenty years, and during this time they continue to suffer and make other people suffer.

Why did the young father not want to talk this thing over with his wife? Because pride got in between them.

Is fighting a conscious decision? Or is it the result of a biological or environmental makeup that we are powerless to control?

Desmond Morris was born in England in 1928 and is a popular British zoologist. Prior to the wide success of his book *The Naked Ape*, published in 1967, Morris worked as a television presenter for *The World of Animals*, *Zoo Time*, and *The Animal Story*. His later works, which include a sequel to *The Naked Ape*, continued to explore human behavior from a zoological perspective.

When *The Naked Ape* was published nearly fifty years ago, it caused an enormous amount of controversy, as it described human beings in the same way as a zoologist portrays animals.

Desmond Morris

from *The Naked Ape*

If we are to understand the nature of our aggressive urges, we must see them against the background of our animal origins. As a species we are so preoccupied with mass-produced and mass-destroying violence at the present time, that we are apt to lose our objectivity when discussing this subject. It is a fact that the most level-headed intellectuals frequently become violently aggressive when discussing the urgent need to suppress aggression. This is not surprising. We are, to put it mildly, in a mess, and there is a strong chance that we shall have exterminated ourselves by the end of the century. Our only consolation will have to be that, as a species, we have had an exciting term of office. Not a long term, as species go, but an amazingly eventful one. But before we examine our own bizarre perfections of attack and defence, we must examine the basic nature of violence in the spearless, gunless, bombless world of animals.

Animals fight amongst themselves for one of two very good reasons: either to establish their dominance in a social hierarchy, or to establish their territorial rights over a particular piece of ground. Some species are purely hierarchical, with no fixed territories. Some are purely territorial, with no hierarchy problems. Some have hierarchies on their territories and have to contend with both forms of aggression. We belong to the last group: we have it both ways. As primates we were already loaded with the hierarchy system.

This is the basic way of primate life. The group keeps moving about, rarely staying anywhere long enough to establish a fixed territory. Occasional inter-group conflict may arise, but it is weakly organized, spasmodic and of comparatively little importance in the life of the average monkey. The "peck order" (so-called because it was first discussed in respect of chickens) is, on the other hand, of vital significance in his day-to-day—and even his minute-to-minute—living. There is a rigidly established social hierarchy in most species of monkeys and apes, with a dominant male in charge of the group, and the others ranged below him in varying degrees of subordination. When he becomes too old or weak to maintain his domination, he is overthrown by a younger, sturdier male, who then assumes the mantle of the colony boss. (In some cases the usurper literally assumes the mantle, growing one in the form of a cape of long hair.) As the troop keeps together all the time, his role as group tyrant is incessantly operative. But despite this he is invariably the sleekest, best-groomed and sexiest monkey in the community.

Although this is a chapter about fighting behaviour, we have so far only dealt with methods of avoiding actual combat. When the situation does finally deteriorate into physical contact, the naked ape—unarmed—behaves in a way that contrasts interestingly with that seen in other primates. For them the teeth are the most important weapons, but for us it is the hands. Where they grab and bite, we grab and squeeze, or strike out with clenched fists. Only in infants or very young children does biting play a significant role in unarmed combat. They, of course, have not yet been able to develop their arm and hand muscles sufficiently to make a great impact with them.

We can witness adult un-armed combat today in a number of highly stylized versions, such as wrestling, judo and boxing, but in its original, unmodified form it is now rare. The moment that serious combat begins, artificial weapons of one sort or another are brought into play. In their crudest form, these are thrown or used as extensions of the fist for delivering heavy blows. Under special circumstances chimpanzees have been able to extend their attacks this far. In conditions of semi-captivity they have been observed to pick up a branch and slam it down hard on to the body of a stuffed leopard, or to tear up clods of earth and hurl them across a water ditch at passers-by. But there is little evidence that they use these methods to any extent in the wild state, and none at all that they use them on one another during disputes between rivals. Nevertheless, they give us a glimpse of the way we probably began, with artificial weapons being developed primarily

SIMON VAN BOOY

as a means of defence against other species and for the killing of prey. Their use in intra-specific fighting was almost certainly a secondary trend, but once the weapons were there, they became available for dealing with any emergency, regardless of the context.

The simplest form of artificial weapon is a hard, solid, but unmodified, natural object of wood or stone. By simple improvements in the shapes of these objects, the crude actions of throwing and hitting became augmented with the addition of spearing, slashing, cutting and stabbing movements.

The next great behavioural trend in attacking methods was the extension of the distance between the attacker and his enemy, and it is this step that has nearly been our undoing. Spears can work at a distance, but their range is too limited. Arrows are better, but they lack accuracy. Guns widen the gap dramatically, but bombs dropped from the sky can be delivered at an even greater range, and ground-to-ground rockets can carry the attacker's "blow" further still. The outcome of this is that the rivals, instead of being defeated, are indiscriminately destroyed. As I explained earlier, the proper business of intra-specific aggression at a biological level is the subduing and not the killing of the enemy. The final stages of destruction of life are avoided because the enemy either flees or submits. In both cases the aggressive encounter is then over: the dispute is settled. But the moment that attacking is done from such a distance that the appeasement signals of the losers cannot be read by the winners, then violent aggression is going to go raging on. It can only be consummated by a direct confrontation with abject submission, or the enemy's headlong flight. Neither of these can be witnessed in the remoteness of modern aggression, and the result is wholesale slaughter on a scale unheard of in any other species.

Aiding and abetting this mayhem is our specially evolved co-operativeness. When we improved this important trait in connection with hunting prey, it served us well, but it has now recoiled upon us. The strong urge towards mutual assistance to which it gave rise has become susceptible to powerful arousal in intra-specific aggressive contexts. Loyalty on the hunt has become loyalty in fighting, and war is born. Ironically, it is the evolution of a deep-seated urge to help our fellows that has been the main cause of all the major horrors of war. It is this that has driven us on and given us our lethal gangs, mobs, hordes and armies. Without it they would lack cohesion and aggression would once again become "personalized."

It has been suggested that because we evolved as specialized prey-killers, we automatically became rival-killers, and that there is an inborn urge within us to murder our opponents. The evidence, as I have already explained, is against this. Defeat is what an animal wants, not murder; domination is the goal of aggression, not destruction, and basically we do not seem to differ from other species in this respect. There is no good reason why we should. What has happened, however, is that because of the vicious combination of attack remoteness and group co-operativeness, the original goal has become blurred for the individuals involved in the fighting. They attack now more to support their comrades than to dominate their enemies, and their inherent susceptibility to direct appeasement is given little or no chance to express itself. This unfortunate development may yet prove to be our undoing and lead to the rapid extinction of the species.

Not unnaturally, this dilemma has given rise to a great deal of displacement head-scratching. A favourite solution is massive mutual disarmament; but to be effective this would have to be carried to an almost impossible extreme, one that would ensure that all future fighting was carried out as close-contact combat where the automatic, direct appeasement signals could come into operation again. Another solution is to de-patriotize the members of the different social groups; but this would be working against a fundamental biological feature of our species. As fast as alliances could be forged in one direction, they would be broken in another. The natural tendency to form social in-groups could never be eradicated without a major genetical change in our make-up, and one which would automatically cause our complex social structure to disintegrate.

A third solution is to provide and promote harmless, symbolic substitutes for war; but if these really are harmless they will inevitably only go a very small way towards resolving the real problem. It is worth remembering here that this problem, at a biological level, is one of group territorial defence and, in view of the gross overcrowding of our species, also one of group territorial expansion. No amount of boisterous international football is going to solve this.

A fourth solution is the improvement of intellectual control over aggression. It is argued that, since our intelligence has got us into this mess, it is our intelligence that must get us out. Unhappily, where matters as basic as territorial defence are concerned, our higher brain centres are all too susceptible to the urgings of our lower ones. Intellectual control can help us just so far, but no further. In the last resort it is unreliable and a single, unreasoned, emotional act can undo all the good it has achieved.

The only sound biological solution to the dilemma is massive de-population, or a rapid spread of the species on to other planets, combined if possible with assistance from all four of the courses of action already mentioned. We already know that if our populations go on increasing at their present terrifying rate, uncontrollable aggressiveness will become dramatically increased. This has been proved conclusively with laboratory experiments. Gross overcrowding will produce

SIMON VAN BOOY

social stresses and tensions that will shatter our community organizations long before it starves us to death. It will work directly against improvements in intellectual control and will savagely heighten the likelihood of emotional explosion. Such a development can be prevented only by a marked drop in the breeding rate. Unfortunately there are two serious snags here. As already explained, the family unit—which is still the basic unit of all our societies—is a rearing device. It has evolved into its present, advanced and complex state as a system for producing, protecting and maturing offspring. If this function is seriously curtailed or temporarily eliminated, the pair-bonding pattern will suffer, and this will bring its own brand of social chaos. If, on the other hand, a selective attempt is made to stem the breeding flood, with certain pairs permitted to breed freely and others prevented from doing so, then this will work against the essential co-operativeness of society.

What it amounts to, in simple numerical terms, is that if all adult members of the population form pairs and breed, they can only afford to produce two offspring per pair if the community is to be maintained at a steady level. Each individual will then, in effect, be replacing him- or herself. Allowing for the fact that a small percentage of the population already fails to mate and breed, and that there will always be a number of premature deaths from accidental injury or other causes, the average family size can, in fact, be slightly larger. Even so, this will put a heavier burden on the pair-bond mechanism. The lighter offspring-load will mean that greater efforts will have to be made in other directions to keep the pair-bonds tightly tied. But this is a much smaller hazard, in the long term, than the alternative of suffocating overcrowding.

To sum up then, the best solution for ensuring world peace is the widespread promotion of contraception or abortion. Abortion is a drastic measure and can involve serious emotional disturbance. Furthermore, once a zygote has been formed by the act of fertilization it constitutes a new individual member of society, and its destruction is, in effect, an act of aggression, which is the very pattern of behaviour that we are attempting to control. Contraception is obviously preferable, and any religious or other "moralizing" factions that oppose it must face the fact that they are engaged in dangerous war-mongering.

I learned long ago, never wrestle with a pig, you get dirty; and besides, the pig likes it.

—*George Bernard Shaw*

Born in 1903 in Vienna, Konrad Lorenz was an animal psychologist, zoologist, and ornithologist. Lorenz credited his scientific career to his parents, who indulged his love for animals as a child. By the age of thirty, he had already earned two doctorates and was studying geese. He joined the Nazi Party in 1938 and became a medic. He was captured by the Russians in 1941, where he continued to work as a medic. After the war, the Russians allowed him to return home with his pet bird and the manuscript of a book he'd been writing. In his later years, Lorenz became an active environmentalist and was awarded the Nobel Prize in 1973. He died in 1989 after authoring over ten important volumes of study, including *On Aggression* (1966), *Civilized Man's Eight Deadly Sins* (1974), *The Year of the Greylag Goose* (1979), and *The Foundations of Ethology* (1982).

Konrad Lorenz

from *On Aggression*

What is the value of all this fighting? In nature, fighting is such an ever-present process, its behavior mechanisms and weapons are so highly developed and have so obviously arisen under the selection pressure of a species-preserving function, that it is our duty to ask this Darwinian question.

The layman, misguided by sensationalism in press and film, imagines the relationship between the various "wild beasts of the jungle" to be a bloodthirsty struggle, all against all. In a widely shown film, a Bengal tiger was seen fighting with a python, and immediately afterward the python with a crocodile. With a clear conscience I can assert that such things never occur under natural conditions. What advantage would one of these animals gain from exterminating the other? Neither of them interferes with the other's vital interests.

Darwin's expression, "the struggle for existence," is sometimes erroneously interpreted as the struggle between different species. In reality, the struggle Darwin was thinking of and which drives evolution forward is the competition between near relations. What causes a species to disappear or become transformed into a different species is the profitable "invention" that falls by chance to one or a few of its members in the everlasting gamble of hereditary change. The descendants of these lucky ones gradually outstrip all others until the particular species consists only of individuals who possess the new "invention."

There are, however, fightlike contests between members of different species: at night an owl kills and eats even well-armed birds of prey, in spite of their vigorous defense, and when these birds meet the owl by day they attack it ferociously. Almost every animal capable of self-defense, from the smallest rodent upward, fights furiously when it is cornered and has no means of escape. Besides these three particular types of inter-specific fighting, there are other, less typical cases; for instance, two cave-nesting birds of different species may fight for a nesting cavity. Something must be said here about these three types of inter-specific fighting in order to explain their peculiarity and to distinguish them from the *intra*-specific aggression which is really the subject of this book.

The survival value of inter-specific fights is much more evident than that of intra-specific contests. The way in which a predatory animal and its prey influence each other's evolution is a classical example of how the selection pressure of a certain function causes corresponding adaptations. The swiftness of the hunted ungulate forces its feline pursuers to evolve enormous leaping power and sharply armed toes. Paleontological discoveries have shown impressive examples of such evolutionary competition between weapons

SIMON VAN BOOY

of attack and those of defense. The teeth of grazing animals have achieved better and better grinding power, while, in their parallel evolution, nutritional plants have devised means of protecting themselves against being eaten, as by the storage of silicates and the development of hard, wooden thorns. This kind of "fight" between the eater and the eaten never goes so far that the predator causes extinction of the prey: a state of equilibrium is always established between them, endurable by both species. The last lions would have died of hunger long before they had killed the last pair of antelopes or zebras; or, in terms of human commercialism, the whaling industry would go bankrupt before the last whales became extinct. What directly threatens the existence of an animal species is never the "eating enemy" but the competitor. In prehistoric times man took the Dingo, a primitive domestic dog, to Australia. It ran wild there, but it did not exterminate a single species of its quarry; instead, it destroyed the large marsupial beasts of prey which ate the same animals as it did itself. The large marsupial predators, the Tasmanian Devil and the Marsupial Wolf, were far superior to the Dingo in strength, but the hunting methods of these "old-fashioned," relatively stupid and slow creatures were inferior to those of the "modern" mammal. The Dingo reduced the marsupial population to such a degree that their methods no longer "paid," and today they exist only in Tasmania, where the Dingo has never penetrated.

In yet another respect the fight between predator and prey is not a fight in the real sense of the word: the stroke of the paw with which a lion kills his prey may resemble the movements that he makes when he strikes his rival, just as a shotgun and a rifle resemble each other outwardly; but the inner motives of the hunter are basically different from those of the fighter. The buffalo which the lion fells provokes his aggression as little as the appetizing turkey which I have just seen hanging in the larder provokes mine. The differences in these inner drives can clearly be seen in the expression movements of the animal: a dog about to catch a hunted rabbit has the same kind of excitedly happy expression as he has when he greets his master or awaits some longed-for treat. From many excellent photographs it can be seen that the lion, in the dramatic moment before he springs, is in no way angry. Growling, laying the ears back, and other well-known expression movements of fighting behavior are seen in predatory animals only when they are very afraid of a wildly resisting prey, and even then the expressions are only suggested.

The opposite process, the "counteroffensive" of the prey against the predator, is more nearly related to genuine aggression. Social animals in particular take every possible chance to attack the "eating enemy" that threatens their safety. This process is called "mobbing." Crows or other birds "mob" a cat or any other nocturnal predator, if they catch sight of it by day.

SIMON VAN BOOY

The survival value of this attack on the eating enemy is self-evident. Even if the attacker is small and defenseless, he may do his enemy considerable harm. All animals which hunt singly have a chance of success only if they take their prey by surprise. If a fox is followed through the wood by a loudly screaming jay, or a sparrow hawk is pursued by a flock of warning wagtails, his hunting is spoiled for the time being. Many birds will mob an owl, if they find one in the daytime, and drive it so far away that it will hunt somewhere else the next night. In some social animals such as jackdaws and many kinds of geese, the function of mobbing is particularly interesting. In jackdaws, its most important survival value is to teach the young, inexperienced birds what a dangerous eating enemy looks like, which they do not know instinctively. Among birds, this is a unique case of traditionally acquired knowledge.

Geese and ducks "know" by very selective, innate releasing mechanisms that anything furry, red-brown, long-shaped, and slinking is extremely dangerous, but nonetheless mobbing, with its intense excitement and the gathering together of geese from far and wide, has an essentially educational character as well as a survival value; anyone who did not know it already learns: foxes may be found *here!* At a time when only part of the shore of our lake was protected by a foxproof fence, the geese kept ten or fifteen yards clear of all unfenced cover likely to conceal a fox, but in the fenced-in area they penetrated fearlessly into the thickets of young fir trees. Besides this didactic function, mobbing of predators by jackdaws and geese still has the basic, original one of making the enemy's life a burden. Jackdaws actively attack their enemy, and geese apparently intimidate it with their cries, their thronging, and their fearless advance. The great Canada geese will even follow a fox over land in a close phalanx, and I have never known a fox in this situation try to catch one of his tormentors. With ears laid back and a disgusted expression on his face, he glances back over his shoulder at the trumpeting flock and trots slowly—so as not to lose face—away from them.

Among the larger, more defense-minded herbivores which, en masse, are a match for even the biggest predators, mobbing is particularly effective; according to reliable reports, zebras will molest even a leopard if they catch him on a veldt where cover is sparse. The reaction of social attack against the wolf is still so ingrained in domestic cattle and pigs that one can sometimes land oneself in danger by going through a field of cows with a nervous dog which, instead of barking at them or at least fleeing independently, seeks refuge between the legs of its owner. Once, when I was out with my bitch Stasi, I was obliged to jump into a lake and swim for safety when a herd of young cattle half encircled us and advanced threateningly; and when he was in southern Hungary during the First World War my brother spent a pleasant afternoon up a tree

SIMON VAN BOOY

with his Scotch terrier under his arm, because a herd of half-wild Hungarian swine, disturbed while grazing in the wood, encircled them, and with bared tusks and unmistakable intentions began to close in on them.

Much more could be said about these effective attacks on the real or supposed enemy. In some birds and fishes, to serve this special purpose brightly colored "aposematic" or warning colors have evolved, which predators notice and associate with unpleasant experiences with the particular species. Poisonous, evil-tasting, or otherwise specially protected animals have, in many cases, "chosen" for these warning signals the combination of red, white, and black; and it is remarkable that the Common Sheldrake and the Sumatra Barb, two creatures which have nothing in common either with each other or the above-named groups, should have done the same thing. It has long been known that Common Sheldrake mob predatory animals and that they so disgust the fox with the sight of their brightly colored plumage that they can nest safely in inhabited foxholes. I bought some Sumatra Barbs because I had asked myself why these fishes looked so poisonous; in a large communal aquarium, they immediately answered my question by mobbing big cichlids so persistently that I had to save the giant predators from the only apparently harmless dwarfs.

There is a third form of fighting behavior, and its survival value is as easily demonstrated as that of the predator's attack on its prey or the mobbing by the prey of the eating enemy. With H. Hediger, we call this third behavior pattern the *critical reaction*. The expression "fighting like a cornered rat" has become symbolic of the desperate struggle in which the fighter stakes his all, because he cannot escape and can expect no mercy. This most violent form of fighting behavior is motivated by fear, by the most intense flight impulses whose natural outlet is prevented by the fact that the danger is too near; so the animal, not daring to turn its back on it, fights with the proverbial courage of desperation. Such a contingency may also occur when, as with the cornered rat, flight is prevented by lack of space, or by strong social ties, like those which forbid an animal to desert its brood or family. The attack which a hen or goose makes on everything that goes too near her chicks or goslings can also be classified as a critical reaction. Many animals will attack desperately when surprised by an enemy at less than a certain critical distance, whereas they would have fled if they had noticed his coming from farther away. As Hediger has described, lion tamers maneuver their great beasts of prey into their positions in the arena by playing a dangerous game with the margin between flight distance and critical distance; and thousands of big game hunting stories testify to the dangerousness of large beasts of prey in dense cover. The reason is that in such circumstances the flight distance is particularly small, because the animal feels safe, imagining that it will not be noticed by a man even if he should penetrate the cover and get quite close; but if in so doing the man oversteps the animal's critical distance, a so-called hunting accident happens quickly and disastrously.

All the cases described above, in which animals of different species fight against each other, have one thing in common: every one of the fighters gains an obvious advantage by its behavior or, at least, in the interests of preserving the species it "ought to" gain one. But intra-specific aggression, aggression in the proper and narrower sense of the word, also fulfills a species-preserving function. Here, too, the Darwinian question "What for?" may and must be asked. Many people will not see the obvious justification for this question, and those accustomed to the classical psychoanalytical way of thinking will probably regard it as a frivolous attempt to vindicate the life-destroying principle or, purely and simply, evil. The average normal civilized human being witnesses aggression only when two of his fellow citizens or two of his domestic animals fight, and therefore sees only its evil effects. In addition there is the alarming progression of aggressive actions ranging from cocks fighting in the barnyard to dogs biting each other, boys thrashing each other, young men throwing beer mugs at each other's heads, and so on to bar-room brawls about politics, and finally to wars and atom bombs.

With humanity in its present cultural and technological situation, we have good reason to consider intra-specific aggression the greatest of all dangers. We shall not improve our chances of counteracting it if we accept it as something metaphysical and inevitable, but on the other hand, we shall perhaps succeed in finding remedies if we investigate the chain of its natural causation. Wherever man has achieved the power of voluntarily guiding a natural phenomenon in a certain direction, he has owed it to his understanding of the chain of causes which formed it. Physiology, the science concerned with the normal life processes and how they fulfill their species-preserving function, forms the essential foundation for pathology, the science investigating their disturbances. Let us forget for a moment that the aggression drive has become derailed under conditions of civilization, and let us inquire impartially into its natural causes. For the reasons already given, as good Darwinians we must inquire into the species-preserving function which, under natural—or rather precultural—conditions, is fulfilled by fights within the species, and which by the process of selection has caused the advanced development of intra-specific fighting behavior in so many higher animals. It is not only fishes that fight their own species: the majority of vertebrates do so too, man included.

Darwin had already raised the question of the survival value of fighting, and he has given us an enlightening answer:

It is always favorable to the future of a species if the stronger of two rivals takes possession either of the territory or of the desired female. As so often, this truth of yesterday is not the untruth of today but only a special case; ecologists have recently demonstrated a much more essential function of aggression. Ecology—derived from the Greek *oikos,* the house—is the branch of biology that deals with the manifold reciprocal relations of the organism to its natural surroundings—its "household"—which of course includes all other animals and plants native to the environment. Unless the special interests of a social organization demand close aggregation of its members, it is obviously most expedient to spread the individuals of an animal species as evenly as possible over the available habitat. To use a human analogy: if, in a certain area, a larger number of doctors, builders, and mechanics want to exist, the representatives of these professions will do well to settle as far away from each other as possible.

The danger of too dense a population of an animal species settling in one part of the available biotope and exhausting all its sources of nutrition and so starving can be obviated by a mutual repulsion acting on the animals of the same species, effecting their regular spacing out, in much the same manner as electrical charges are regularly distributed all over the surface of a spherical conductor. This, in plain terms, is the most important survival value of intra-specific aggression.

Now we can understand why the sedentary coral fish in particular are so crazily colored. There are few biotopes on earth that provide so much and such varied nutrition as a coral reef. Here fish species can, in an evolutionary sense, take up very different professions: one can support itself as an "unskilled laborer," doing what any average fish can do, hunting creatures that are neither poisonous nor armor-plated nor prickly, in other words hunting all the defenseless organisms approaching the reef from the open sea, some as "plankton," others as active swimmers "intending" to settle on the reef, as millions of free-swimming larvae of all coral-dwelling organisms do. On the other hand, another fish species may specialize in eating forms of life that live on the reef itself and are therefore equipped with some sort of protective mechanism which the hunting fish must render harmless. Corals themselves provide many different kinds of nourishment for a whole series of fish species. Pointed-jawed butterfly fish get their food parasitically from corals and other stinging animals. They search continuously in the coral stems for small prey caught in the stinging tentacles of coral polyps. As soon as they see these, they produce, by fanning with their pectoral fins, a current so directly aimed at the prey that at the required point a "parting" is made between the polyps, pressing their tentacles flat on all sides and thus enabling the fish to seize the prey almost without getting its nose stung. It always gets it just a little stung and can be seen "sneezing" and shaking its nose, but, like pepper, the sting seems to act as an agreeable stimulant. My beautiful yellow and brown butterfly fishes prefer a prey, such as a piece of fish, stuck in the tentacles of a stinging sea anemone, to the same prey swimming free in the water. Other related species have developed a stronger immunity to stings and they devour the prey together with the coral animal that has caught it. Yet other species disregard the stinging capsules of coelenterates altogether, and eat coral animals, hydroid polyps, and even big, strong, stinging sea anemones, as placidly as a cow eats grass. As well as this immunity to poison, parrot fish have evolved a strong chisellike dentition and they eat whole branches of coral including their calcareous skeleton. If you dive near a grazing herd of these beautiful, rainbow-colored fish, you can hear a cracking and crunching as though a little gravel mill were at work—and this actually corresponds with the facts, for when such a fish excretes, it rains a little shower of white sand, and the observer realizes with astonishment that most of the snow-clean coral sand covering the glades of the coral forest has obviously passed through parrot fish.

Other fish, plectognaths, to which the comical puffers, runk, and porcupine fish belong, have specialized in cracking hard-shelled mollusks, crabs, and sea urchins; and others again, such as angelfish, specialize in snatching the lovely feather crowns that certain feather worms thrust out of their hard, calcareous tubes. Their capacity for quick retraction acts as a protection against slower predators, but some angelfish have a way of sidling up and, with a lightning sideways jerk of the mouth, seizing the worm's head at a speed surpassing its capacity for withdrawal. Even in the aquarium, where they seize prey which has no such quick reactions, these fish cannot do otherwise than snap like this.

The reef offers many other "openings" for specialized fish. There are some which remove parasites from others and which are therefore left unharmed by the fiercest predators, even when they penetrate right into the mouth cavities of their hosts to perform their hygienic work. There are others which live as parasites on large fish, punching pieces from their epidermis, and among these are the oddest fish of all: they resemble the cleaner fish so closely in color, form, and movement that, under false pretenses, they can safely approach their victims.

It is essential to consider the fact that all these opportunities for special careers, known as ecological niches, are often provided by the same cubic yard of ocean water. Because of the enormous nutritional possibilities, every fish, whatever its specialty, requires only a few square yards of sea bottom for its support, so in this small area there can be as many fish as there are ecological niches, and anyone who has watched with amazement the thronging traffic on a coral reef knows that these are legion. However, every one of this crowd is determined that no other fish of his species should settle in his territory. Specialists of other "professions" harm his livelihood as little as, to use our analogy again, the practice of a doctor harms the trade of a mechanic living in the same village.

In less densely populated biotopes where the same unit of space can support three or four species only, a resident fish or bird can "afford" to drive away all living beings, even members of species that are no real threat to his existence; but if a sedentary coral fish tried to do the same thing, it would be utterly exhausted and, moreover, would never manage to keep its territory free from the swarms of noncompetitors of different "professions." It is in the occupational interests of all sedentary species that each should determine the spatial distribution that will benefit its own individuals, entirely without consideration for other species. The colorful "poster" patterns, described in Chapter One, and the fighting reactions elicited by them, have the effect that the fish of each species keep a measured distance only from nutritional competitors of the same species. This is the very simple answer to the much discussed question of the function of the colors of coral fish.

As I have already mentioned, the species-typical song of birds has a very similar survival value to that of the visual signals of fishes. From the song of a certain bird, other birds not yet in possession of a territory recognize that in this particular place a male is proclaiming territorial rights. It is remarkable that in many species the song indicates how strong and possibly how old the singer is, in other words, how much the listener has to fear him. Among several species of birds that mark their territory acoustically, there is great individual difference of sound expression, and some observers are of the opinion that, in such species, the personal visiting card is of special significance. While Heinroth interpreted the crowing of the cock with the words, "Here is a cock!" Baeumer, the most knowledgeable of all domestic-fowl experts, heard in it the far more special announcement, "Here is the cock Balthazar!"

Among mammals, which mostly "think through their noses," it is not surprising that marking of the territory by scent plays a big role. Many methods have been tried; various scent glands have been evolved, and the most remarkable ceremonies developed around the depositing of urine and feces; of these the leg-lifting of the domestic dog is the most familiar. The objection has been raised by some students of mammals that such scent marks cannot have anything to do with territorial ownership because they are found not only in socially living mammals which do not defend single territories, but also in animals that wander far and wide; but this opinion is only partly correct. First, it has been proved that

SIMON VAN BOOY

dogs and other pack-living animals recognize each other by the scent of the marks, and it would at once be apparent to the members of a pack if a nonmember presumed to lift its leg in their hunting grounds. Secondly, Leyhausen and Wolf have demonstrated the very interesting possibility that the distribution of animals of a certain species over the available biotope can be effected not only by a space plan but also by a time plan. They found that, in domestic cats living free in open country, several individuals could make use of the same hunting ground without ever coming into conflict, by using it according to a definite timetable, in the same way as our Seewiesen housewives use our communal washhouse. An additional safeguard against undesirable encounters is the scent marks which these animals—the cats, not the housewives—deposit at regular intervals wherever they go. These act like railway signals whose aim is to prevent collision between two trains. A cat finding another cat's signal on its hunting path assesses its age, and if it is very fresh it hesitates, or chooses another path; if it is a few hours old it proceeds calmly on its way.

Even in the case of animals whose territory is governed by space only, the hunting ground must not be imagined as a property determined by geographical confines; it is determined by the fact that in every individual the readiness to fight is greatest in the most familiar place, that is, in the middle of its territory.

In other words, the threshold value of fight-eliciting stimuli is at its lowest where the animal feels safest, that is, where its readiness to fight is least diminished by its readiness to escape. As the distance from this "headquarters" increases, the readiness to fight decreases proportionately as the surroundings become stranger and more intimidating to the animal. If one plotted the graph of this decrease the curve would not be equally steep for all directions in space. In fish, the center of whose territory is nearly always on the bottom, the decline in readiness to fight is most marked in the vertical direction because the fish is threatened by special dangers from above.

The territory which an animal apparently possesses is thus only a matter of variations in readiness to fight, depending on the place and on various local factors inhibiting the fighting urge. In nearing the center of the territory the aggressive urge increases in geometrical ratio to the decrease in distance from this center. This increase in aggression is so great that it compensates for all differences ever to be found in adult, sexually mature animals of a species. If we know the territorial centers of two conflicting animals, such as two garden redstarts or two aquarium sticklebacks, all other things being equal, we can predict, from the place of encounter, which one will win: the one that is nearer home.

When the loser flees, the inertia of reaction of both animals leads to that phenomenon which always occurs when a time lag enters into a self-regulating process—to an oscillation. The courage of the fugitive returns as he nears his own headquarters, while that of the pursuer sinks in proportion to the distance covered in enemy territory. Finally the fugitive turns and attacks the former pursuer vigorously and unexpectedly and, as was predictable, he in his turn is beaten and driven away. The whole performance is repeated several times till both fighters come to a standstill at a certain point of balance where they threaten each other without fighting.

The position, the territorial "border," is in no way marked on the ground but is determined exclusively by a balance of power and may, if this alters in the least, for instance if one fish is replete and lazy, come to lie in a new position somewhat nearer the headquarters of the lazy one. An old record of our observations on the territorial behavior of two pairs of cichlids demonstrates this oscillation of the territorial borders. Four fish of this species were put into a large tank and at once the strongest male, A, occupied the left, back, lower corner and chased the other three mercilessly around the whole tank; in other words, he claimed the whole tank as his territory. After a few days, male B took possession of a tiny space immediately below the surface in the diagonally opposite right, front, upper corner. There he bravely resisted the attacks of the first male. This occupation of an area near the surface is in a way an act of desperation for one of these fish, because it is risking great danger from aerial predators in order to hold its own against an enemy of its own species, which, as already explained, will attack less resolutely in such a locality. In other words, the owner of such a dangerous area has, as an ally, the fear which the surface inspires in its bad neighbor. During succeeding days, the space defended by B grew visibly, expanding downward until he finally took his station in the right, front, lower corner, so gaining a much more satisfactory headquarters. Now at last he had the same chances as A, whom he quickly pressed so far back that their territories divided the tank into two almost equal parts. It was interesting to see how both fishes patrolled the border continuously, maintaining a threatening attitude. Then one morning they were doing this on the extreme right of the tank, again around the original headquarters of B, who could now scarcely call a few square inches his own. I knew at once what had happened: A had paired, and since it is characteristic of all large cichlids that both partners take part in territorial defense, B was subjected to double pressure and his territory had decreased accordingly. Next day the fish were again in the middle of the tank, threatening each other across the "border," but now there were four, because B had also taken a mate, and thus the balance of power with the A family was restored. A week later I found the border far toward the left lower area, and encroaching on A's former territory. The reason for this was that the A couple had spawned and since one of the partners was busy looking after the eggs, only one at a time was able to attend to frontier defense. As soon as the B couple had also spawned, the previous equal division of space was re-established. Julian Huxley once used a good metaphor to describe this behavior: he compared the territories to air-balloons in a closed container, pressing against each other and expanding or contracting with the slightest change of pressure in each individual one. This territorial aggression, really a very simple mechanism of behavior-physiology, gives an ideal solution to the problem of the distribution of animals of any one species over the available area in such a way that it is favorable to the species as a whole. Even the weaker specimens can exist and reproduce, if only in a very small space. This has special significance in creatures which reach sexual maturity long before they are fully grown. What a peaceful issue of the "evil principle"!

In many animals the same result is achieved without aggressive behavior. Theoretically it suffices that animals of the same species "cannot bear the smell of each other" and avoid each other accordingly. To a certain extent this applies to the smell signals deposited by cats, though behind these lies a hidden threat of active aggression. There are some vertebrates which entirely lack intra-specific aggression but which nevertheless avoid their own species meticulously. Some frogs, in particular tree frogs, live solitary lives except at mating time, and they are obviously distributed very evenly over the available habitat. As American scientists have recently discovered, this distribution is effected quite simply by the fact that every frog avoids the quacking sound of his own species. This explanation, however, does not account for the distribution of the females, for these, in most frogs, are dumb.

We can safely assume that the most important function of intra-specific aggression is the even distribution of the animals of a particular species over an inhabitable area, but it is certainly not its only one. Charles Darwin had already observed that sexual selection, the selection of the best and strongest animals for reproduction, was furthered by the fighting of rival animals, particularly males. The strength of the father directly affects the welfare of the children in those species in which he plays an active part in their care and defense. The correlation between male parental care and rival fighting is clear, particularly in those animals which are not territorial in the sense which the cichlids demonstrate but which wander more or less nomadically, as, for example, large ungulates, ground apes, and many others. In such animals, intra-specific aggression plays no essential part in the "spacing out" of the species. Bisons, antelopes, horses, etc., form large herds, and territorial borders and territorial jealousy are unknown to them since there is enough food for all. Nevertheless the males of these species fight each other violently and dramatically, and there is no doubt that the selection resulting from this aggressive behavior leads to the evolution of particularly strong and courageous defenders of family and herd; conversely, there is just as little doubt that the survival value of herd defense has resulted in selective breeding for hard rival fights. This interaction has produced impressive fighters such as bull bison or the males of the large baboon species; at every threat to the community, these valiantly surround and protect the weaker members of the herd.

In connection with rival fights attention must be drawn to a fact which, though it seems paradoxical to the nonbiologist, is, as we shall show later on in this book, of the very greatest importance: purely intra-specific selective breeding can lead to the development of forms and behavior patterns which are not only nonadaptive but can even have adverse effects on species preservation. This is why, in the last paragraph, I emphasized the fact that family defense, a form of strife with the extra-specific environment, has evolved the rival fight, and this in its turn has developed the powerful males. If sexual rivalry, or any other form of intra-specific competition, exerts selection pressure uninfluenced by any environmental exigencies, it may develop in a direction which is quite unadaptive to environment, and irrelevant, if not positively detrimental, to survival. This process may give rise to bizarre physical forms of no use to the species. The antlers of stags, for example, were developed in the service of rival fights, and a stag without them has little hope of producing progeny. Otherwise antlers are useless, for male stags defend themselves against beasts of prey with their fore-hoofs only and never with their antlers. Only the reindeer has based an invention on this necessity and "learned" to shovel snow with a widened point of its antlers.

Sexual selection by the female often has the same results as the rival fights. Wherever we find exaggerated development of colorful feathers, bizarre forms, etc., in the male, we may suspect that the males no longer fight but that the last word in the choice of a mate is spoken by the female, and that the male has no means of contesting this decision. Birds of Paradise, the Ruff, the Mandarin Duck, and the Argus Pheasant show examples of such behavior. The Argus hen pheasant reacts to the large secondary wing feathers of the cock; they are decorated with beautiful eye spots and the cock spreads them before her during courtship. They are so huge that the cock can scarcely fly, and the bigger they are the more they stimulate the hen. The number of progeny produced by a cock in a certain period of time is in direct proportion to the length of these feathers, and, even if their extreme development is unfavorable in other ways—his unwieldiness may cause him to be eaten by a predator while a rival with less absurdly exaggerated wings may escape—he will nevertheless leave more descendants than will a plainer cock. So the predisposition to

SIMON VAN BOOY

huge wing feathers is preserved, quite against the interests of the species. One could well imagine an Argus hen that reacted to a small red spot on the wings of the male, which would disappear when he folded his wings and interfere neither with his flying capacity nor with his protective color, but the evolution of the Argus pheasant has run itself into a blind alley. The males continue to compete in producing the largest possible wing feathers, and these birds will never reach a sensible solution and "decide" to stop this nonsense at once.

Here for the first time we are up against a strange and almost uncanny phenomenon. We know that the techniques of trial and error used by the great master builders sometimes lead inevitably to plans that fall short of perfect efficiency. In the plant and animal worlds there are, besides the efficient, quantities of characteristics which only just avoid leading the particular species to destruction. But in the case of the Argus pheasant we have something quite different: it is not only like the strict efficiency expert "closing an eye" and letting second-rate construction pass in the interests of experiment, but it is selection itself that has here run into a blind alley which may easily result in destruction. This always happens when competition between members of a species causes selective breeding without any relation to the extra-specific environment.

My teacher, Oskar Heinroth, used to say jokingly, "Next to the wings of the Argus pheasant, the hectic life of Western civilized man is the most stupid product of intra-specific selection!" The rushed existence into which industrialized, commercialized man has precipitated himself is actually a good example of an inexpedient development caused entirely by competition between members of the same species. Human beings of today are attacked by so-called manager diseases, high blood pressure, renal atrophy, gastric ulcers, and torturing neuroses; they succumb to barbarism because they have no more time for cultural interests. And all this is unnecessary, for they could easily agree to take things more easily; theoretically they could, but in practice it is just as impossible for them as it is for the Argus pheasant to grow shorter wing feathers.

There are still worse consequences of intra-specific selection, and for obvious reasons man is particularly exposed to them: unlike any creature before him, he has mastered all hostile powers in his environment, he has exterminated the bear and the wolf and now, as the Latin proverb says, *"Homo homini lupus."* Striking support for this view comes from the work of modern American sociologists, and in his book *The Hidden Persuaders* Vance Packard gives an impressive picture of the grotesque state of affairs to which commercial competition can lead. Reading this book, one is tempted to believe that intra-specific competition is the "root of all evil" in a more direct sense than aggression can ever be.

In this chapter on the survival value of aggression, I have laid special stress on the potentially destructive effects of intra-specific selection: because of them, aggressive behavior can, more than other qualities and functions, become exaggerated to the point of the grotesque and inexpedient. In later chapters we shall see what effects it has had in several animals, for example, in the Egyptian Goose and the Brown Rat. Above all, it is more than probable that the destructive intensity of the aggression drive, still a hereditary evil of mankind, is the consequence of a process of intra-specific selection which worked on our forefathers for roughly forty thousand years, that is, throughout the Early Stone Age. When man had reached the stage of having weapons, clothing, and social organization, so overcoming the dangers of starving, freezing, and being eaten by wild animals, and these dangers ceased to be the essential factors influencing selection, an evil intra-specific selection must have set in. The factor influencing selection was now the wars waged between hostile neighboring tribes. These must have evolved in an extreme form of all those so-called "warrior virtues" which unfortunately many people still regard as desirable ideals. We shall come back to this in the last chapter of this book.

I return to the theme of the survival value of the rival fight, with the statement that this only leads to useful selection where it breeds fighters fitted for combat with extra-specific enemies as well as for intra-specific duels. The most important function of rival fighting is the selection of an aggressive family defender, and this presupposes a further function of intra-specific aggression: brood defense. This is so obvious that it requires no further comment. If it should be doubted, its truth can be demonstrated by the fact that in many animals, where only one sex cares for the brood, only that sex is really aggressive toward fellow members of the species. Among sticklebacks it is the male, in several dwarf cichlids the female. In many gallinaceous birds, only the females tend the brood, and these are often far more aggressive than the males. The same thing is said to be true of human beings.

It would be wrong to believe that the three functions of aggressive behavior dealt with in the last three chapters—namely, balanced distribution of animals of the same species over the available environment, selection of the strongest by rival fights, and defense of the young—are its only important functions in the preservation of the species. We shall see later what an indispensable part in the great complex of drives is played by aggression; it is one of those driving powers which students of behavior call "motivation"; it lies behind behavior patterns that outwardly have nothing to do with aggression, and even appear to be its very opposite. It is hard to say whether it is a paradox or a commonplace that, in the most intimate bonds between living creatures, there is a certain measure of aggression. Much more remains to be said before discussing this central problem in our natural history of aggression. The important part played by aggression in the interaction of drives within the organism is not easy to understand and still less easy to expound.

We can, however, here describe the part played by aggression in the structure of society among highly developed animals. Though many individuals interact in a social system, its inner workings are often easier to understand than the interaction of drives within the individual. A principle of organization without which a more advanced social life cannot develop in higher vertebrates is the so-called ranking order. Under this rule every individual in the society knows which one is stronger and which weaker than itself, so that everyone can retreat from the stronger and expect submission from the weaker, if they should get in each other's way. Schjelderup-Ebbe was the first to examine the ranking order in the domestic fowl and to speak of the "pecking order," an expression used to this day by writers. It seems a little odd though, to me, to speak of a pecking order even for large animals which certainly do not peck, but bite or ram. However, its wide distribution speaks for its great survival value, and therefore we must ask wherein this lies.

The most obvious answer is that it limits fighting between the members of a society, but here in contrast one may ask:

Would it not have been better if aggression among members of a society were utterly inhibited? To this, a whole series of answers can be given. First, as we shall discuss very thoroughly in a later chapter (Ten, "The Bond"), the case may arise that a society, for example, a wolf pack or monkey herd, urgently needs aggression against other societies of the same species, therefore aggression should be inhibited only *inside* the horde. Secondly, a society may derive a beneficial firmness of structure from the state of tension arising inside the community from the aggression drive and its result, ranking order. In jackdaws, and in many other very social birds, ranking order leads directly to protection of the weaker ones. All social animals are "status seekers," hence there is always particularly high tension between individuals who hold immediately adjoining positions in the ranking order; conversely, this tension diminishes the further apart the two animals are in rank. Since high-ranking jackdaws, particularly males, interfere in every quarrel between two inferiors, this graduation of social tension has the desirable effect that the higher-ranking birds always intervene in favor of the losing party.

In jackdaws, another form of "authority" is already linked with the ranking position which the individual has acquired by its aggressive drive. The expression movements of a high-ranking jackdaw, particularly of an old male, are given much more attention by the colony members than those of a lower-ranking, young bird. For example, if a young bird shows fright at some meaningless stimulus, the others, especially the older ones, pay almost no attention to his expressions of fear. But if the same sort of alarm proceeds from one of the old males, all the jackdaws within sight and earshot immediately take flight. Since, in jackdaws, recognition of predatory enemies is not innate but is learned by every individual from the behavior of experienced old birds, it is probably of considerable importance that great store is set by the "opinion" of old, high-ranking, and experienced birds.

With the higher evolution of an animal species, the significance of the role played by individual experience and learning generally increases, while innate behavior, though not losing importance, becomes reduced to simpler though not less numerous elements. With this general trend in evolution, the significance attached to the experienced old animal becomes greater all the time, and it may even be said that the social coexistence of intelligent mammals has achieved a new survival value by the use it makes of the handing down of individually acquired information. Conversely, it may be said that social coexistence exerts selection pressure in the direction of better learning capacity, because in social animals this faculty benefits not only the individual but also the community. Thus longevity far beyond the age of reproductive capacity has considerable species-preserving value. We know from Fraser

Darling and Margaret Altmann that in many species of deer the herd is led by an aged female, no longer hampered in her social duties by the obligations of motherhood.

All other conditions being equal, the age of an animal is, very consistently, in direct proportion to the position it holds in the ranking order of its society. It is thus advantageous if the "constructors" of behavior rely upon this consistency and if the members of the community—who cannot read the age of the experienced leader animal in its birth certificate—rate its reliability by its rank. Some time ago, collaborators of Robert M. Yerkes made the extraordinarily interesting observation that chimpanzees, animals well known to be capable of learning by imitation, copy only higher-ranking members of their species. From a group of these apes, a low-ranking individual was taken and taught to remove bananas from a specially constructed feeding apparatus by very complicated manipulations. When this ape, together with his feeding apparatus, was brought back to the group, the higher-ranking animals tried to take away the bananas which he had acquired for himself, but none of them thought of watching their inferior at work and learning something from him. Then the highest-ranking chimpanzee was removed and taught to use the apparatus in the same way, and when he was put back in the group the other members watched him with great interest and soon learned to imitate him.

S. L. Washburn and Irven de Vore observed that among free-living baboons the band was led not by a single animal but by a "senate" of several old males who maintained their superiority over the younger and physically stronger members by firmly sticking together and proving, as a united force, stronger than any single young male. In a more exactly observed case, one of the three "senators" was seen to be an almost toothless old creature while the other two were well past their prime. On one occasion when the band was in a treeless area and in danger of encountering a lion, the animals stopped and the young, strong males formed a defensive circle around the weaker animals. But the oldest male went forward alone, performed the dangerous task of finding out exactly where the lion was lying, without being seen by him, and then returned to the horde and led them, by a wide detour around the lion, to the safety of their sleeping trees. All followed him blindly, no one doubting his authority.

Let us look back on all that we have learned in this chapter from the objective observation of animals, and consider in what ways intra-specific aggression assists the preservation of an animal species. The environment is divided between the members of the species in such a way that, within the potentialities offered, everyone can exist. The best father, the best mother are chosen for the benefit of the progeny. The children are protected. The community is so organized that a few wise males, the "senate," acquire the authority essential for making and carrying out decisions for the good of the community. Though occasionally, in territorial or rival fights, by some mishap a horn may penetrate an eye or a tooth an artery, we have never found that the aim of aggression was the extermination of fellow members of the species concerned. This of course does not negate the fact that under unnatural circumstances, for example confinement, unforeseen by the "constructors" of evolution, aggressive behavior may have a destructive effect.

Let us now examine ourselves and try, without self-conceit but also without regarding ourselves as miserable sinners, to find out what we would like to do, in a state of highest violent aggressive feeling, to the person who elicited that emotion. I do not think I am claiming to be better than I am when I say that the final, drive-assuaging act, Wallace Craig's consummatory act, is not the killing of my enemy. The satisfying experience consists, in such cases, in administering a good beating, but certainly not in shooting or disemboweling; and the desired objective is not that my opponent should lie dead but that he should be soundly thrashed and humbly accept my physical and, if I am to be considered as good as a baboon, my mental superiority. And since, on principle, I only wish to thrash such fellows as deserve these humiliations, I cannot entirely condemn my instincts in this connection. However, it must be admitted that a slight deviation from nature, a coincidence that put a knife into one's hand at the critical moment, might turn an intended thrashing into manslaughter.

Summing up what has been said in this chapter, we find that aggression, far from being the diabolical, destructive principle that classical psychoanalysis makes it out to be, is really an essential part of the life-preserving organization of instincts. Though by accident it may function in the wrong way and cause destruction, the same is true of practically any functional part of any system. Moreover, we have not yet considered an all-important fact which we shall hear about in Chapter Ten. Mutation and selection, the great "constructors" which make genealogical trees grow upward, have chosen, of all unlikely things, the rough and spiny shoot of intra-specific aggression to bear the blossoms of personal friendship and love.

Very little of the great cruelty shown by men can really be attributed to cruel instinct. Most of it comes from thoughtlessness or inherited habit.

 —*Albert Schweitzer from* Memoirs of Childhood and Youth

Richard Leakey was born in 1944 and is a paleoan-thropologist, conservationist, and Kenyan politician. At school, Leakey (who, like his father, favored racial integration) was bullied severely for his beliefs. At sixteen, he left school and became a successful busi-nessman by starting a safari business after obtaining a pilot's license. He has authored several important books, and is Chair of the Turkana Basin Institute, at Stony Brook University in New York.

Roger Lewin, a British anthropologist and author of twenty books, collaborated with Leakey on *Origins* and two other books.

In this extract from "Aggression, Sex, and Human Nature" from *Origins: The Emergence and Evolution of Our Species and Its Possible Future*, Leakey and Lewin argue that the *seeds* of war may not lie solely in our genes.

Roger Lewin

"Aggression, Sex, and Human Nature" from *Origins*

Human babies, it is fair to say, arrive in the world virtually devoid of functionally useful instincts, apart from the so-called rooting reflex and the sucking response: the baby turns its head towards the nipple and sucks. Even here, the baby's experience within its mother's womb can affect the way it later sucks at the nipple, showing the response to be more than a basic, immutable mechanism. Within a day or two after birth the baby can recognize the smell of its mother's milk. And within a week or so it has matched the sound of a familiar voice with a familiar face, showing that the long career of human learning starts very early. The rules for human behavior are therefore very simple: as each of us is a highly-sophisticated and intelligent piece of biological machinery, our responses will be finely tuned to our environment; experience and learning help us to tune these responses, but extreme experience may over-emphasize particular forms of behavior—a child reared in a home which stresses physical punishment is more than normally likely to grow up physically aggressive.

The rules for human behavior are simple, we believe, precisely because they offer such a wide scope for expression. By contrast, the proponents of innate aggression try to tie us down to narrow, well-defined paths of behavior: humans are aggressive, they propose, because there is a universal territorial instinct in biology; territories are established and maintained by displays of aggression; our ancestors acquired weapons, turning ritual displays into bloody combat, a development that was exacerbated through a lust for killing. And according to the Lorenzian school, aggression is such a crucial part of the territorial animal's survival kit that it is backed up by a steady rise in pressure for its expression. Aggression may be released by an appropriate cue, such as a threat by another animal, but in the protracted absence of such cues the pressure eventually reaches a critical point at which the behavior bursts out spontaneously. The difference between a piece of behavior that is elicited by a particular type of stimulus, and one that will be expressed whether or not cues occur is enormous, and that difference is central to understanding aggression in the human context.

There is no doubt that aggression and territoriality are part of modern life: vandalism is a distressingly familiar mark of the urban scene; we lock the doors of our houses and apartments against strangers who might wander in; and there is war, an apparent display of territoriality and aggression on a grand scale. Are these unsavory aspects of modern living simply part of an inescapable legacy of our animal origins? Or are they phenomena with entirely different causes? These are the questions that must be answered since they are so clearly relevant to the future of our species.

To begin with, it is worth taking a broad view of territoriality and aggression in the animal world. Why are some animals territorial? Simply to protect resources, such as food, a nest, or a similar reproductive area. Many birds defend one piece of real estate in which a male may attract and court a female, and then move off to another one, also to be defended, in which they build a nest and rear young. The "choking" by male kittiwakes, the lunging by sticklebacks, and the early morning chorus by gibbons are all displays announcing ownership of territory. Intruders who persist in violating another's territory are soon met with such displays, the intention of which is quite clear. The clarity of the defender's response, and also of the intruder's prowess, is the secret of nature's success with these so-called aggressive encounters.

Such confrontations are strictly ritualized, so that on all but the rarest occasions the biologically fitter of the two wins without the infliction of physical damage on either one. This "aggression" is in fact an exercise in competitive display rather than physical violence. The individuals engage in stereotyped lunges, thrusts, and postures which may or may not be similar to their responses when a real threat to their lives arises, as from a predator for instance. In either event, the outcome is a resolution of a territorial dispute with minimal injury to either party. The biological advantage of these mock battles is clear: a species that insists on settling disputes violently reduces its overall fitness to thrive in a world that offers enough environmental challenges anyway.

The biological common sense implicit in this simple behavioral device is reiterated again and again throughout the animal kingdom, and even as far down as some ants: disputes over territorial ownership, and over sexual rights too, are channeled into stereotyped, non-violent competitions. This law is so deeply embedded in the nature of survival and success in the game of evolution that for a species to transgress, there must be extremely unusual circumstances. We cannot deny that with the invention of tools, first made of wood and later of stone, an impulse to employ them occasionally as weapons might have caused serious injury, there being no stereotype behavior patterns to deflect this risk. And it is possible that our increasingly intelligent ancestors may have understood the implications of power over others through the delivery of one swift blow with a sharpened pebble tool. But is it likely?

The answer must be no. An animal that develops a proclivity for killing its fellows thrusts itself into an evolutionarily disadvantageous position. Because our ancestors probably lived in small bands, in which individuals were closely related to one another, and had as neighbors similar bands which also contained blood relations, in most acts of murder the victim would more than likely have been kin to the murderer. As the evolutionary success is the production of as many descendants as possible, an innate drive for killing individuals of one's own species would soon have wiped that species out. Humans, as we know, did not blunder up an evolutionary blind alley, a fate that innate, unrestrained aggressiveness would undoubtedly have produced.

To argue, as we do, that humans are innately non-aggressive toward one another is not to imply that we are of necessity innately good-natured toward our fellows. In the lower echelons of the animal kingdom the management of conflict is largely through ritualized mock battles. But farther along the evolutionary path, carrying out the appropriate avoidance behavior comes to depend more and more on learning, and in social animals the channel of learning is social education. The capacity for that behavior is rooted in the animal's genes, but its elaboration depends also on learning. And, as we have stressed, humans are learning animals par excellence, so we must expect that techniques for coping with potential conflict are largely learned.

For instance, among the Polynesian Ifaluk of the western Pacific, real violence is so thoroughly condemned that "ritual" management of conflict is taught in childhood. The children play boisterously, as any normal children do; however a child who feels that he or she is being treated unfairly will set off in pursuit of the offender—but at a pace that will not permit catching up. As other children stand around, showing looks of disapproval, the chase may end with the plaintiff throwing pieces of coconut at the accused—once again with sufficient care so as to miss the target! This is ritual conflict, but it is not stereotyped human behavior. It is culturally based, not genetic. And the result is a very peaceable society.

An example of ritual conflict among adults comes from the Kurelu people in the heart of New Guinea. Superficially these people would seem to be engaged in frequent tribal warfare. But instead of pursuing that warfare to its undoubted lethal potential, they fire arrows at one another from a distance just outside the range of the weapons. Occasionally people are injured but far less often than would be inevitable if they were intent on a serious confrontation.

The ritualized nature of animals' conflict over territory is therefore the first major point to be made concerning aggression. That humans can likewise engage in ritual conflict emphasizes the biological good sense of the procedure, but does not imply that it is rooted in our genes. Humans are not innately disposed powerfully either to aggression or to peace. It is culture that largely weaves the patterns in human societies.

A second crucial feature of animal conflict is its variability. It occurs, that is to say, both between animals of different species and between individuals of the same species, and under differing environmental conditions. Anyone who argues for inbuilt aggression in *Homo sapiens* must see aggression as a universal instinct in the animal kingdom. It is no such thing. Much of the research on territoriality and aggression concerns birds. Because they usually must build nests, in which they will then spend a good deal of time incubating eggs, and still longer rearing their young, it is a biological necessity for them to protect their territory. If they did not their offspring would perish, and that ultimately implies the extinction of the species. It is therefore not surprising that most birds possess a strong territorial drive. But simply because greylag geese and mockingbirds, for instance, enthusiastically defend their territory, we should not infer that all animals do so. And it is not surprising that hummingbirds show considerably more territorial aggression than lions, even though the king of beasts is a lethal hunter. Our closest animal relatives, the chimpanzees and gorillas, are notably nonterritorial. Both these species are relatively mobile, even when there are young within the group, and they can forage for food over a wide area. Gibbons, though acrobatic, are not inclined to travel far; hence their need to stake out a territory, since it will contain their food supply.

The animal kingdom therefore offers a broad spectrum of territoriality, whose basic determining factor is the mode of reproduction and style of daily life. Indeed, an animal may find it necessary to assert ownership of land in one situation and not in another. Thus, the ayu, a salm-onoid fish, is territorial in shallow water, whereas in deep pools it moves in close and harmonious company with its fellows. And vervet monkeys in the crowded Lolui Island of Uganda are aggressively territorial, but at Chobe, just a few miles away, animals of this species live much more equable lives; the reason is that there they have more space with no population problem.

That territoriality is flexible should not be surprising. It is, after all, a biological adaption to environmental conditions so that the species may survive through sufficient access to food supplies and by unhampered reproduction. If food resources and space are scarce, then almost certainly there will be con-spicuous territorial behavior. It is likewise inevitable that some individuals will fail to secure sufficient food or a place in which to rear a brood. These individuals are, of course, the weakest, and this is what survival of the fittest through natural selec-tion really means. The pressure for selection applies with force only when resources are limited—in other words, when there is a good biological reason.

Territorial behavior is therefore triggered when it is re-quired and remains dormant when it is not. The Lorenzians, however, take a different view: aggression, they say, builds up inexorably, to be released either by appropriate cues or spontaneously in the absence of cues at all. A safety valve suggested by Lorenzians for human societies is competitive sport. But such a suggestion neglects the high correlation between highly competitive encounters and associated vandalism and physical violence—as players, referees, and crowds know to their cost through Europe and the Americas. More significantly, research now shows a close match between warlike behavior in countries and a devotion to sport. Far from defusing aggression, highly-organized, emotionally-charged sporting events generate even more aggression and reflect the degree to which humans' deep propensity to group identity and cohesion can be manipulated.

We can say therefore that territoriality and aggression are not universal instincts as such. Rather they are pieces of behavior that are tuned to particular life styles and to changes in the availability of important resources in the environment. This being said, it follows rationally that at times of environmental stress our ancestors must have found themselves forced into territorial behavior of some kind, presumably involving competition between groups for whatever resources were limited at the time. Lorenz writes that part of such stress for early humans would have come from "the counter-pressures of hostile neighboring hordes"—an image more dramatically evocative than it is based in fact.

SIMON VAN BOOY

．　　　．　　　．

Altogether, then, the notion that humans are inherently aggressive is simply not tenable. We cannot deny that twentieth-century humans display a good deal of aggression, but we cannot point to our evolutionary past either to explain its origins, or to excuse it. For that is what the equating of territorial aggressiveness in the animal domain with waging war in the human one often amounts to—an excuse. The fallacy of thus adducing our animal origins should now be evident. Wars are planned and organized by leaders intent on increasing their power. And they are fought usually by people not driven by an innate aggression against an enemy they often do not see. In war men are more like sheep than wolves: they may be led to manufacture munitions at home, to release bombs, or to fire long-range guns and rockets—all as part of one great cooperative effort. It is not insignificant that those soldiers who engage in fierce and bloody hand-to-hand fighting are subjected to an intense process of desensitization before they can do it.

War is a battle for power over people and for resources such as land and minerals, neither of which are relevant in hunting and gathering societes. With the growth of agriculture and of materially-based societies, warfare has increased steadily in both ferocity and duration, culminating in our current capability to destroy even the planet: powerful leaders have found more and more to fight about, and increasingly effective ways of achieving their ends. We should not look to our genes for the seeds of war; those seeds were planted when, ten thousand years ago, our ancestors for the first time planted crops and began to be farmers. The transition from the nomadic hunting way of life to the sedentary one of farmers and industrialists made war possible and potentially profitable.

Possible, but not inevitable. For what has transformed the possible into reality is the same factor that has made human beings special in the biological kingdom: culture. Because of our seemingly limitless inventiveness and our vast capacity for learning, there is an endless potential for difference among human cultures, as indeed may be witnessed throughout the world. An essential element of culture, however, consists in those central values that make up an ideology. It is social and political ideologies, and the tolerance or lack of it between them, that bring human nations to bloody conflict. Those who argue that war is in our genes not only are wrong, but they also commit the crime of diverting attention from the real cause of war.

This last criticism applies even more strongly to those who cite innate aggression to explain violence within nations, particularly in the overcrowded urban areas. There are many reasons why a youth may "spontaneously" smash a window or attack an old lady, but an inborn drive inherited from our animal origins is certainly not one of them. Human behavior is extraordinarily sensitive to the nature of the environment, and so it should not be particularly surprising that a person reared in unpleasant surroundings, perhaps subjected to material insecurity and emotional deprivation, should later behave in a way that people blessed with a more fortunate life might regard as unpleasant. Urban problems will not be solved by pointing to supposed defects in our genes while ignoring real defects in social justice.

Poverty is the mother of crime.

—*Marcus Aurelius*

Victor Hugo was born in 1802 and wanted to be a writer from an early age. Hugo was extremely prolific, and his first complete novel, *The Hunchback of Notre Dame*, published in 1831, was an enormous success. One effect of the novel's popularity was to force the city of Paris to restore the crumbling Notre Dame Cathedral, due to the amount of tourism generated by the book. *Les Miserables* took Hugo seventeen years to write and was published in 1862. When he died in 1885, two million people made up his funeral procession.

In Hugo's *Les Miserables*, the main character, Jean Valjean, is changed from a good-natured, hardworking man into a hardened criminal when he spends nineteen years in prison because of his decision to steal bread to feed his starving sister and her kids.

Victor Hugo

from *Les Miserables*

CHAPTER VI—JEAN VALJEAN

Towards the middle of the night Jean Valjean woke.

Jean Valjean came from a poor peasant family of Brie. He had not learned to read in his childhood. When he reached man's estate, he became a tree-pruner at Faverolles. His mother was named Jeanne Mathieu; his father was called Jean Valjean or Vlajean, probably a sobriquet, and a contraction of voilà Jean, "here's Jean."

Jean Valjean was of that thoughtful but not gloomy disposition which constitutes the peculiarity of affectionate natures. On the whole, however, there was something decidedly sluggish and insignificant about Jean Valjean in appearance, at least. He had lost his father and mother at a very early age. His mother had died of a milk fever, which had not been properly attended to. His father, a tree-pruner, like himself, had been killed by a fall from a tree. All that remained to Jean Valjean was a sister older than himself,—a widow with seven children, boys and girls. This sister had brought up Jean Valjean, and so long as she had a husband she lodged and fed her young brother.

The husband died. The eldest of the seven children was eight years old. The youngest, one.

Jean Valjean had just attained his twenty-fifth year. He took the father's place, and, in his turn, supported the sister who had brought him up. This was done simply as a duty and even a little churlishly on the part of Jean Valjean. Thus his youth had been spent in rude and ill-paid toil. He had never known a "kind woman friend" in his native parts. He had not had the time to fall in love.

He returned at night weary, and ate his broth without uttering a word. His sister, mother Jeanne, often took the best part of his repast from his bowl while he was eating,—a bit of meat, a slice of bacon, the heart of the cabbage,—to give to one of her children. As he went on eating, with his head bent over the table and almost into his soup, his long hair falling about his bowl and concealing his eyes, he had the air of perceiving nothing and allowing it. There was at Faverolles, not far from the Valjean thatched cottage, on the other side of the lane, a farmer's wife named Marie-Claude; the Valjean children, habitually famished, sometimes went to borrow from Marie-Claude a pint of milk, in their mother's name, which they drank behind a hedge or in some alley corner, snatching the jug from each other so hastily that the little girls spilled it on their aprons and down their necks. If their mother had known of this marauding, she would have punished the delinquents severely. Jean Valjean gruffly and grumblingly paid Marie-Claude for the pint of milk behind their mother's back, and the children were not punished.

In pruning season he earned eighteen sous a day; then he hired out as a hay-maker, as laborer, as neat-herd on a farm, as a drudge. He did whatever he could. His sister worked also but what could she do with seven little children? It was a sad group enveloped in misery, which was being gradually annihilated. A very hard winter came. Jean had no work. The family had no bread. No bread literally. Seven children!

One Sunday evening, Maubert Isabeau, the baker on the Church Square at Faverolles, was preparing to go to bed, when he heard a violent blow on the grated front of his shop. He arrived in time to see an arm passed through a hole made by a blow from a fist, through the grating and the glass. The arm seized a loaf of bread and carried it off. Isabeau ran out in haste; the robber fled at the full speed of his legs. Isabeau ran after him and stopped him. The thief had flung away the loaf, but his arm was still bleeding. It was Jean Valjean.

This took place in 1795. Jean Valjean was taken before the tribunals of the time for theft and breaking and entering an inhabited house at night. He had a gun which he used better than any one else in the world, he was a bit of a poacher, and this injured his case. There exists a legitimate prejudice against poachers. The poacher, like the smuggler, smacks too strongly of the brigand. Nevertheless, we will remark cursorily, there is still an abyss between these races of men and the hideous assassin of the towns. The poacher lives in the forest, the smuggler lives in the mountains or on the sea. The cities make ferocious men because they make corrupt men. The mountain, the sea, the forest, make savage men; they develop the fierce side, but often without destroying the humane side.

Jean Valjean was pronounced guilty. The terms of the Code were explicit. There occur formidable hours in our civilization; there are moments when the penal laws decree a shipwreck. What an ominous minute is that in which society draws back and consummates the irreparable abandonment of a sentient being! Jean Valjean was condemned to five years in the galleys.

On the 22d of April, 1796, the victory of Montenotte, won by the general-in-chief of the army of Italy, whom the message of the Directory to the Five Hundred, of the 2d of Floreal, year IV, calls Buona-Parte, was announced in Paris; on that same day a great gang of galley-slaves was put in chains at Bicetre. Jean Valjean formed a part of that gang. An old turnkey of the prison, who is now nearly eighty years old, still recalls perfectly that unfortunate wretch who was chained to the end of the fourth line, in the north angle of the courtyard. He was seated on the ground like the others. He did not seem to comprehend his position, except that it was horrible. It is probable that he, also, was disentangling from amid the vague ideas of a poor man, ignorant of everything, something excessive. While the bolt of his iron collar was being riveted behind his head with heavy blows from the hammer, he wept, his tears stifled him, they impeded his speech; he only managed to say from time to time, "I was a tree-pruner at Faverolles." Then still sobbing, he raised his right hand and lowered it gradually seven times, as though he were touching in succession seven heads of unequal heights, and from this gesture it was divined that the thing which he had done, whatever it was, he had done for the sake of clothing and nourishing seven little children.

He set out for Toulon. He arrived there, after a journey of twenty-seven days, on a cart, with a chain on his neck. At Toulon he was clothed in the red cassock. All that had constituted his life, even to his name, was effaced; he was no longer even Jean Valjean; he was number 24,601. What became of his sister? What became of the seven children? Who troubled himself about that? What becomes of the handful of leaves from the young tree which is sawed off at the root?

It is always the same story. These poor living beings, these creatures of God, henceforth without support, without guide, without refuge, wandered away at random,—who even knows?—each in his own direction perhaps, and little by little buried themselves in that cold mist which engulfs solitary destinies; gloomy shades, into which disappear in succession so many unlucky heads, in the sombre march of the human race. They quitted the country. The clock-tower of what had been their village forgot them; the boundary line of what had been their field forgot them; after a few years' residence in the galleys, Jean Valjean himself forgot them. In that heart, where there had been a wound, there was a scar. That is all. Only once, during all the time which he spent at Toulon, did he hear his sister mentioned. This happened, I think, towards the end of the fourth year of his captivity. I know not through what channels the news reached him. Some one who had known them in their own country had seen his sister. She was in Paris. She lived in a poor street rear Saint-Sulpice, in the Rue du Gindre. She had with her only one child, a little boy, the youngest. Where were the other six? Perhaps she did not know herself. Every morning she went to a printing office, No. 3 Rue du Sabot, where she was a folder and stitcher. She was obliged to be there at six o'clock in the morning— long before daylight in winter. In the same building with the printing office there was a school, and to this school she took her little boy, who was seven years old. But as she entered the printing office at six, and the school only opened at seven, the child had to wait in the courtyard, for the school to open, for an hour—one hour of a winter night in the open air! They would not allow the child to come into the printing office, because he was in the way, they said. When the workmen passed in the morning, they beheld this poor little being seated on the pavement, overcome with drowsiness, and often fast asleep in the shadow, crouched down and doubled up over his basket. When it rained, an old woman, the portress, took pity on him; she took him into her den, where there was a pallet, a spinning-wheel, and two wooden chairs, and the little one slumbered in a corner, pressing himself close to the cat that he might suffer less from cold. At seven o'clock the school opened, and he entered. That is what was told to Jean Valjean.

They talked to him about it for one day; it was a moment, a flash, as though a window had suddenly been opened upon the destiny of those things whom he had loved; then all closed again. He heard nothing more forever. Nothing from them ever reached him again; he never beheld them; he never met them again; and in the continuation of this mournful history they will not be met with any more.

Towards the end of this fourth year Jean Valjean's turn to escape arrived. His comrades assisted him, as is the custom in that sad place. He escaped. He wandered for two days in the fields at liberty, if being at liberty is to be hunted, to turn the head every instant, to quake at the slightest noise, to be afraid of everything,—of a smoking roof, of a passing man, of a barking dog, of a galloping horse, of a striking clock, of the day because one can see, of the night because one cannot see, of the highway, of the path, of a bush, of sleep. On the evening of the second day he was captured. He had neither eaten nor slept for thirty-six hours. The maritime tribunal condemned him, for this crime, to a prolongation of his term for three years, which made eight years. In the sixth year his turn to escape occurred again; he availed himself of it, but could not accomplish his flight fully. He was missing at roll-call. The cannon were fired, and at night the patrol found him hidden under the keel of a vessel in process of construction; he resisted the galley guards who seized him. Escape and rebellion. This case, provided for by a special code, was punished by an addition of five years, two of them in the double chain. Thirteen years. In the tenth year his turn came round again; he again profited by it; he succeeded no better. Three years for this fresh attempt. Sixteen years. Finally, I think it was during his thirteenth year, he made a last attempt, and only succeeded in getting retaken at the end of four hours of absence. Three years for those four hours. Nineteen years. In October, 1815, he was released; he had entered there in 1796, for having broken a pane of glass and taken a loaf of bread.

Room for a brief parenthesis. This is the second time, during his studies on the penal question and damnation by law, that the author of this book has come across the theft of a loaf of bread as the point of departure for the disaster of a destiny. Claude Gueux had stolen a loaf; Jean Valjean had stolen a loaf. English statistics prove the fact that four thefts out of five in London have hunger for their immediate cause.

Jean Valjean had entered the galleys sobbing and shuddering; he emerged impassive. He had entered in despair; he emerged gloomy.

What had taken place in that soul?

CHAPTER VII—THE INTERIOR OF DESPAIR

Let us try to say it.

It is necessary that society should look at these things, because it is itself which creates them.

He was, as we have said, an ignorant man, but he was not a fool. The light of nature was ignited in him. Unhappiness, which also possesses a clearness of vision of its own, augmented the small amount of daylight which existed in this mind. Beneath the cudgel, beneath the chain, in the cell, in hardship, beneath the burning sun of the galleys, upon the plank bed of the convict, he withdrew into his own consciousness and meditated.

He constituted himself the tribunal.

He began by putting himself on trial.

He recognized the fact that he was not an innocent man unjustly punished. He admitted that he had committed an extreme and blameworthy act; that that loaf of bread would probably not have been refused to him had he asked for it; that, in any case, it would have been better to wait until he could get it through compassion or through work; that it is not an unanswerable argument to say, "Can one wait when one is hungry?" That, in the first place, it is very rare for any one to die of hunger, literally; and next, that, fortunately or unfortunately, man is so constituted that he can suffer long and much, both morally and physically, without dying; that it is therefore necessary to have patience; that that would even have been better for those poor little children; that it had been an act of madness for him, a miserable, unfortunate wretch, to take society at large violently by the collar, and to imagine that one can escape from misery through theft; that that is in any case a poor door through which to escape from misery through which infamy enters; in short, that he was in the wrong.

Then he asked himself—

Whether he had been the only one in fault in his fatal history. Whether it was not a serious thing, that he, a laborer, out of work, that he, an industrious man, should have lacked bread. And whether, the fault once committed and confessed, the chastisement had not been ferocious and disproportioned. Whether there had not been more abuse on the part of the law, in respect to the penalty, than there had been on the part of the culprit in respect to his fault. Whether there had not been an excess of weights in one balance of the scale, in the one which contains expiation. Whether the over-weight of the penalty was not equivalent to the annihilation of the crime, and did not result in reversing the situation, of replacing the fault of the delinquent by the fault of the repression, of converting the guilty man into the victim, and the debtor into the creditor, and of ranging the law definitely on the side of the man who had violated it.

Whether this penalty, complicated by successive aggravations for attempts at escape, had not ended in becoming a sort of outrage perpetrated by the stronger upon the feebler, a crime of society against the individual, a crime which was being committed afresh every day, a crime which had lasted nineteen years.

He asked himself whether human society could have the right to force its members to suffer equally in one case for its own unreasonable lack of foresight, and in the other case for its pitiless foresight; and to seize a poor man forever between a defect and an excess, a default of work and an excess of punishment.

Whether it was not outrageous for society to treat thus precisely those of its members who were the least well endowed in the division of goods made by chance, and consequently the most deserving of consideration.

These questions put and answered, he judged society and condemned it.

He condemned it to his hatred.

He made it responsible for the fate which he was suffering, and he said to himself that it might be that one day he should not hesitate to call it to account. He declared to himself that there was no equilibrium between the harm which he had caused and the harm which was being done to him; he finally arrived at the conclusion that his punishment was not, in truth, unjust, but that it most assuredly was iniquitous.

Anger may be both foolish and absurd; one can be irritated wrongfully; one is exasperated only when there is some show of right on one's side at bottom. Jean Valjean felt himself exasperated.

And besides, human society had done him nothing but harm; he had never seen anything of it save that angry face which it calls Justice, and which it shows to those whom it strikes. Men had only touched him to bruise him. Every contact with them had been a blow. Never, since his infancy, since the days of his mother, of his sister, had he ever encountered a friendly word and a kindly glance. From suffering to suffering, he had gradually arrived at the conviction that life is a war; and that in this war he was the conquered. He had no other weapon than his hate. He resolved to whet it in the galleys and to bear it away with him when he departed.

As one reads history, not in the expurgated editions written for schoolboys and passmen, but in the original authorities of each time, one is absolutely sickened, not by the crimes that the wicked have committed, but by the punishments that the good have inflicted; and a community is infinitely more brutalised by the habitual employment of punishment than it is by the occasional occurrence of crime.

—*Oscar Wilde from* The Soul of Man Under Socialism

The jury, passing on the prisoner's life,
May in the sworn twelve have a thief or two
Guiltier than him they try.

—*William Shakespeare from* Measure for Measure

German painter and sculptor Käthe Schmidt Kollwitz was born in 1867 and is famous for the empathy evoked by her unique form of expressionism. In 1891 she married Karl Kollwitz, a doctor who took care of Berlin's poorest residents. Subjects in higher social realms were uninteresting to Kollwitz as an artist, and she found the greatest beauty in the struggle of the poor.

Kollwitz was a pacifist and a socialist, so when Hitler rose to power, she was forced to resign her faculty position at the Academy in Kunste. Her work was also removed from German museums. When the Gestapo visited her in 1936 and threatened to send her to a concentration camp, she and her husband planned to commit suicide if such a fate became unavoidable. Kollwitz, however, was world famous, so no further action was taken against her. She died in 1945.

Käthe Schmidt Kollwitz, *Poverty,* 1893

Charles Dickens was born in 1812, in the British city of Portsmouth. When Dickens was twelve, his father was sent to prison for non-payment of debts. This forced young Dickens to work ten-hour days in a factory, putting labels on tubs of shoe polish. Eventually, an inheritance allowed Dickens's father to leave prison, but his mother kept her son at the factory. By 1836, however, Dickens was working as a political journalist, traveling around Britain by stagecoach to cover stories and events. Throughout his literary career, Dickens wrote about his firsthand experience of the wretched treatment of children, and was an outspoken advocate for labor and social reform. His work provides a detailed cross section of British life and the social classes of the time, while also being a brilliant record of the vernacular used in Victorian Britain. He died in 1870 at home.

In his novel, *Oliver Twist*, the main characters of the story appear to have been driven to social deviance because society has failed to provide for their basic human needs. They fight not because they want to, but because they have no choice if they are to survive in an unfair, underserved society.

Charles Dickens

from *Oliver Twist*

For a long time, Oliver remained motionless in this attitude. The candle was burning low in the socket when he rose to his feet. Having gazed cautiously round him, and listened intently, he gently undid the fastenings of the door, and looked abroad.

It was a cold, dark night. The stars seemed, to the boy's eyes, farther from the earth than he had ever seen them before; there was no wind; and the sombre shadows thrown by the trees upon the ground, looked sepulchral and death-like, from being so still. He softly reclosed the door. Having availed himself of the expiring light of the candle to tie up in a handkerchief the few articles of wearing apparel he had, he sat himself down upon a bench to wait for morning.

With the first ray of light that struggled through the crevices in the shutters, Oliver arose, and again unbarred the door. One timid look around—one moment's pause of hesitation—he had closed it behind him, and was in the open street.

He looked to the right and to the left, uncertain whither to fly. He remembered to have seen the waggons, as they went out, toiling up the hill. He took the same route; and arriving at a footpad, across the fields; which he knew, after some distance, led out again into the road; struck into it, and walked quickly on.

Along this same footpath, Oliver well remembered he had trotted beside Mr. Bumble, when he first carried him to the workhouse from the farm. His way lay directly in front of the cottage. His heart beat quickly when he bethought himself of this; and he half resolved to turn back. He had come a long way though, and should lose a great deal of time by doing so. Besides, it was so early that there was very little fear of his being seen: so he walked on.

He reached the house. There was no appearance of its inmates stirring at that early hour. Oliver stopped, and peeped into the garden. A child was weeding one of the little beds; as he stopped he raised his pale face and disclosed the features of one of his former companions. Oliver felt glad to see him, before he went for, though younger than himself, he had been his little friend and playmate. They had been beaten, and starved, and shut up together, many and many a time.

"Hush, Dick!" said Oliver, as the boy ran to the gate, and thrust his thin arm between the rails to greet him. "Is any one up?"

"Nobody but me," replied the child.

"You mustn't say you saw me, Dick," said Oliver. "I am running away. They beat and ill-use me, Dick; and I am going to seek my fortune, some long way off. I don't know where. How pale you are!"

"I heard the doctor tell them I was dying," replied the child with a faint smile. "I am very glad to see you, dear; but don't stop, don't stop!"

"Yes, yes, I will, to say good-b'ye to you," replied Oliver. "I shall see you again, Dick. I know I shall! You will be well and happy!"

"I hope so," replied the child. "After I am dead, but not before. I know the doctor must be right, Oliver, because I dream so much of Heaven, and Angels, and kind faces that I never see when I am awake. Kiss me," said the child, climbing up the low gate, and flinging his little arms round Oliver's neck. "Good-b'ye, dear! God bless you!"

The blessing was from a young child's lips, but it was the first that Oliver had ever heard invoked upon his head; and through the struggles and sufferings, and troubles and changes, of his after life, he never once forgot it.

CHAPTER VIII—OLIVER WALKS TO LONDON. HE ENCOUNTERS ON THE ROAD A STRANGE SORT OF YOUNG GENTLEMAN.

Oliver reached the stile at which the bypath terminated; and once more gained the highroad. It was eight o'clock now. Though he was nearly five miles away from the town, he ran, and hid behind the hedges, by turns, till noon: fearing that he might be pursued and overtaken. Then he sat down to rest by the side of the milestone, and began to think, for the first time, where he had better go and try to live.

The stone by which he was seated, bore, in large characters, an intimation that it was just seventy miles from that spot to London. The name awakened a new train of ideas in the boy's mind. London!—that great large place!—nobody—not even Mr. Bumble—could ever find him there! He had often heard the old men in the workhouse, too, say that no lad of spirit need want in London: and that there were ways of living in that vast city, which those who had been bred up in country parts had no idea of. It was the very place for a homeless boy, who must die in the streets unless some one helped him. As these things passed through his thoughts, he jumped upon his feet, and again walked forward.

He had diminished the distance between himself and London by full four miles more, before he recollected how much he must undergo ere he could hope to reach his place of destination. As this consideration forced itself upon him, he slackened his pace a little, and meditated upon his means of getting there. He had a crust of bread, a coarse shirt, and two pairs of stockings, in his bundle. He had a penny too—a gift of Sowerberry's after some funeral in which he had acquitted himself more than ordinarily well—in his pocket. "A clean shirt," thought Oliver, "is a very comfortable thing; and so are two pairs of darned stockings; and so is a penny: but they are small helps to a sixty-five miles' walk in winter time." But Oliver's thoughts, like those of most other people, although

SIMON VAN BOOY

they were extremely ready and active to point out his difficulties, were wholly at a loss to suggest any feasible mode of surmounting them; so, after a good deal of thinking to no particular purpose, he changed his little bundle over to the other shoulder, and trudged on.

Oliver walked twenty miles that day: and all that time tasted nothing but the crust of dry bread, and a few draughts of water, which he begged at the cottage-doors by the roadside. When the night came, he turned into a meadow; and, creeping close under a hayrick, determined to lie there, till morning. He felt frightened at first, for the wind moaned dismally over the empty fields: and he was cold and hungry, and more alone than he had ever felt before. Being very tired with his walk, however, he soon fell asleep and forgot his troubles.

He felt cold and stiff, when he got up next morning, and so hungry that he was obliged to exchange the penny for a small loaf, in the very first village through which he passed. He had walked no more than twelve miles, when night closed in again. His feet were sore, and his legs so weak that they trembled beneath him. Another night passed in the bleak damp air, made him worse; when he set forward on his journey next morning, he could hardly crawl along.

He waited at the bottom of a steep hill till a stage-coach came up, and then begged of the outside passengers: but there were very few who took any notice of him: and even those told him to wait till they got to the top of the hill, and then let them see how far he could run for a halfpenny. Poor Oliver tried to keep up with the coach a little way, but was unable to do it, by reason of his fatigue and sore feet. When the outsides saw this, they put their halfpence back into their pockets again, declaring that he was an idle young dog, and didn't deserve anything; and the coach rattled away and left only a cloud of dust behind.

In some villages, large painted boards were fixed up: warning all persons who begged within the district, that they would be sent to jail. This frightened Oliver very much, and made him glad to get out of those villages with all possible expedition. In others, he would stand about the inn-yards, and look mournfully at every one who passed: a proceeding which generally terminated in the landlady's ordering one of the post-boys who were lounging about, to drive that strange boy out of the place, for she was sure he had come to steal something. If he begged at a farmer's house, ten to one but they threatened to set the dog on him; and when he showed his nose in a shop, they talked about the beadle—which brought Oliver's heart into his mouth,—very often the only thing he had there, for many hours together.

In fact, if it had not been for a good-hearted turnpike-man, and a benevolent old lady, Oliver's troubles would have been shortened by the very same process which had put an end to his mother's; in other words, he would most assuredly have fallen dead upon the king's highway. But the turnpike-man gave him a meal of bread and cheese: and the old lady, who had a shipwrecked grandson wan-dering barefoot in some distant part of the earth, took pity upon the poor orphan, and gave him what little she could afford—and more—with such kind and gentle words, and such tears of sympathy and compassion, thatthey sank deeper into Oliver's soul, than all the sufferingshe had ever undergone.

Early on the seventh morning after he had left his native place, Oliver limped slowly into the little town of Barnet. The window-shutters were closed; the street was empty; not a soul had awakened to the business of the day. The sun was rising in all its splendid beauty; but the light only served to show the boy his own lonesomeness and desolation, as he sat, with bleeding feet and covered with dust, upon a door-step.

By degrees, the shutters were opened; the window-blinds were drawn up; and people began passing to and fro. Some few stopped to gaze at Oliver for a moment or two, or turned round to stare at him as they hurried by; but none relieved him, or troubled themselves to inquire how he came there. He had no heart to beg. And there he sat.

He had been crouching on the step for some time: wondering at the great number of public-houses (every other house in Barnet was a tavern, large or small), gazing listlessly at the coaches as they passed through, and thinking how strange it seemed that they could do, with ease, in a few hours, what it had taken him a whole week of courage and determination beyond his years to accomplish: when he was roused by observing that a boy, who had passed him carelessly some minutes before, had returned, and was now surveying him most earnestly from the opposite side of the way. He took little heed of this at first; but the boy remained in the same attitude of close observation so long, that Oliver raised his head, and returned his steady look. Upon this, the boy crossed over; and, walking close up to Oliver, said.

"Hullo, my covey! What's the row?"

The boy who addressed this inquiry to the young wayfarer, was about his own age: but one of the queerest looking boys that Oliver had ever seen. He was a snub-nosed, flat-browed, common-faced boy enough; and as dirty a juvenile as one would wish to see; but he had about him all the airs and manners of a man. He was short of his age: with rather bow-legs, and little, sharp, ugly eyes. His hat was stuck on the top of his head so lightly, that it threatened to fall off every moment—and would have done so, very often, if the wearer had not had a knack of every now and then giving his head a sudden twitch, which brought it back to its old place again. He wore a man's coat, which reached nearly to his heels. He had turned the cuffs back, half-way up his arm, to get his hands out of the sleeves: apparently with the ultimate view of thrusting them into the pockets of his corduroy trousers: for there he kept them. He was, altogether, as roystering and swaggering a young gentleman as ever stood four feet six, or something less, in his bluchers.

"Hullo, my covey! What's the row?" said this strange young gentleman to Oliver.

"I am very hungry and tired," replied Oliver: the tears standing in his eyes as he spoke. "I have walked a long way. I have been walking these seven days."

"Walking for sivin days!" said the young gentleman. "Oh I see. Beak's order, eh? But," he added, noticing Oliver's look of surprise. "I suppose you don't know what a beak is, my flash compan-i-on."

Oliver mildly replied, that he had always heard a bird's mouth described by the term in question.

"My eyes, how green!" exclaimed the young gentleman. "Why, a beak's a madgst'rate; and when you walk by a beak's order, it's not straight forerd, but always agoing up, and nivir a coming down agin. Was you never on the mill?"

"What mill?" inquired Oliver.

"What mill! Why, *the* mill—the mill as takes up so little room that it'll work inside a Stone Jug; and always goes better when the wind's low with people, than when it's high; acos then they can't get workmen. But come," said the young gentleman; "you want grub, and you shall have it. I'm at low-watermark myself—

only one bob and a magpie; but, *as* far *as* it goes, I'll fork out and stump. Up with you on your pins. There! Now then! Morrice!"

Assisting Oliver to rise, the young gentleman took him to an adjacent chandler's shop, where he purchased a sufficiency of ready-dressed ham and a half-quartern loaf, or, as he himself expressed it, "a fourpenny bran!" the ham being kept clean and preserved from dust, by the ingenious expedient of making a hole in the loaf by pulling out a portion of the crumb, and stuffing it therein. Taking the bread under his arm, the young gentleman turned into a small public-house, and led the way to a tap-room in the rear of the premises. Here, a pot of beer was brought in, by direction of the mysterious youth; and Oliver, falling to, at his new friend's bidding, made a long and hearty meal, during the progress on which, the strange boy eyed him from time to time with great attention.

"Going to London?" said the strange boy, when Oliver had at length concluded.

"Yes."

"Got any lodgings?"

"No."

"Money?"

"No."

The strange boy whistled; and put his arms into his pockets, as far as the big coat sleeves would let them go.

"Do you live in London?" inquired Oliver.

"Yes. I do, when I'm at home," replied the boy. "I suppose you want some place to sleep in to-night, don't you?"

"I do, indeed," answered Oliver. "I have not slept under a roof since I left the country."

"Don't fret your eyelids on that score," said the young gentleman. "I've got to be in London to-night; and I know a 'spectable old genelman as lives there, wot'll give you lodgings for nothink, and never ask for the change—that is, if any genelman he knows interduces you. And don't he know me? Oh, no! Not in the least! By no means. Certainly not!"

The young gentleman smiled, as if to intimate that the latter fragments of discourse were playfully ironical; and finished the beer as he did so.

This unexpected offer of shelter was too tempting to be resisted: especially as it was immediately followed up, by the assurance that the old gentleman referred to, would doubtless provide Oliver with a comfortable place, without loss of time. This led to a more friendly and confidential dialogue; from which Oliver discovered that his friend's name was Jack Dawkins, and that he was a peculiar pet and *protégé* of the elderly gentleman before mentioned.

Mr. Dawkins's appearance did not say a vast deal in favour of the comforts which his patron's interest obtained for those whom he took under his protection; but, as he had a rather flighty and dissolute mode of conversing, and furthermore avowed that among his intimate friends he was better known by the *sobriquet* of "The artful Dodger," Oliver concluded that, being of a dissipated and careless turn, the moral precepts of his benefactor had hitherto been thrown away upon him. Under this impression, he secretly resolved to cultivate the good opinion of the old gentleman as quickly as possible; and, if he found the Dodger incorrigible, as he more than half suspected he should, to decline the honour of his farther acquaintance.

As John Dawkins objected to their entering London before nightfall, it was nearly eleven o'clock when they reached the turnpike at Islington. They crossed from the Angel into St. John's Road; struck down the small street which terminates at Sadler's Wells Theatre; through Exmouth Street and Coppice Row; down the little court by the side of the workhouse; across the classic ground which once bore the name of Hockley-in-the-Hole; thence into Little Saffron Hill; and so into Saffron Hill the Great; along which the Dodger scudded at a rapid pace, directing Oliver to follow close at his heels.

Although Oliver had enough to occupy his attention in keeping sight of his leader, he could not help bestowing a few hasty glances on either side of the way, as he passed along. A dirtier or more wretched place he had never seen. The street was very narrow and muddy, and the air was impregnated with filthy odours. There were a good many small shops; but the only stock in trade appeared to be heaps of

SIMON VAN BOOY

children, who, even at that time of night, were crawling in and out at the doors, or screaming from the inside. The sole places that seemed to prosper amid the general blight of the place, were the public-houses; and in them, the lowest orders of Irish were wrangling with might and main. Covered ways and yards, which here and there diverged from the main street, disclosed little knots of houses, where drunken men and women were positively wallowing in filth; and from several of the doorways, great ill-looking fellows were cautiously emerging, bound, to all appearance, on no very well-disposed or harmless errands.

Oliver was just considering whether he hadn't better run away, when they reached the bottom of the hill. His conductor, catching him by the arm, pushed open the door of a house near Field Lane; and, drawing him into the passage, closed it behind him.

"Now, then!" cried a voice from below, in reply to a whistle from the Dodger.

"Plummy and slam!" was the reply.

This seemed to be some watchword or signal that all was right; for the light of a feeble candle gleamed on the wall at the remote end of the passage; and a man's face peeped out, from where a balustrade of the old kitchen staircase had been broken away.

"There's two on you," said the man, thrusting the candle farther out, and shading his eyes with his hand. "Who's the t'other one?"

"A new pal," replied Jack Dawkins, pulling Oliver forward.

"Where did he come from?"

"Greenland: Is Fagin upstairs?"

"Yes, he's a sortin' the wipes. Up with you!" The candle was drawn back, and the face disappeared.

Oliver, groping his way with one hand, and having the other firmly grasped by his companion, ascended with much difficulty the dark and broken stairs: which his conductor mounted with an ease and expedition that showed he was well acquainted with them. He threw open the door of a back-room, and drew Oliver in after him.

The walls and ceiling of the room were perfectly black with age and dirt. There was a deal table before the fire: upon which were a candle, stuck in a ginger-beer bottle, two or three pewter pots, a loaf and butter, and a plate. In a frying-pan, which was on the fire, and which was secured to the mantelshelf by a string, some sausages were cooking; and standing over them, with a toasting-fork in his hand, was a very old shrivelled Jew, whose villainous-looking and repulsive face was obscured by a quantity of matted red hair. He was dressed in a greasy flannel gown, with his throat bare; and seemed to be dividing his attention between the frying-pan and a clothes-horse, over which a great number of silk hand-kerchiefs were hanging. Several rough beds made of old sacks were huddled side by side on the floor. Seated round the table were four or five boys, none older than the Dodger, smoking long clay pipes, and drinking spirits with the air of middle-aged men. These all crowded about their associate as he whispered a few words to the Jew; and then turned round and grinned at Oliver. So did the Jew himself, toasting-fork in hand.

"This is him, Fagin," said Jack Dawkins; "my friend Oliver Twist."

The Jew grinned; and, making a low obeisance to Oliver, took him by the hand, and hoped he should have the honour of his intimate acquaintance. Upon this, the young gentleman with the pipes came round him, and shook both his hands very hard—especially the one in which he held his little bundle. One young gentleman was very anxious to hang up his cap for him; and another was so obliging as to put his hands in his pockets, in order that, as he was very tired, he might not have the trouble of emptying them, himself, when he went to bed. These civilities would probably have been extended much farther, but for a liberal exercise of the Jew's toasting-fork on the heads and shoulders of the affectionate youths who offered them.

"We are very glad to see you, Oliver, very," said the Jew. "Dodger, take off the sausages; and draw a tub near the fire for Oliver. Ah, you're a-staring at the pocket-handkerchiefs! eh, my dear. There are a good many of 'em, ain't there? We've just looked 'em out, ready for the wash; that's all, Oliver; that's all. Ha! ha! ha!"

The latter part of this speech, was hailed by a boisterous shout from all the hopeful pupils of the merry old gentleman. In the midst of which they went to supper.

Oliver ate his share, and the Jew then mixed him a glass of hot gin-and-water: telling him he must drink it off directly, because another gentleman wanted the tumbler. Oliver did as he was desired. Immediately afterwards he felt himself gently lifted on to one of the sacks; and then he sunk into a deep sleep.

CHAPTER IX—CONTAINING FURTHER PARTICULARS CONCERNING THE PLEASANT OLD GENTLEMAN, AND HIS HOPEFUL PUPILS.

It was late next morning when Oliver awoke, from a sound, long sleep. There was no other person in the room but the old Jew, who was boiling some coffee in a saucepan for breakfast, and whistling softly to himself as he stirred it round and round, with an iron spoon. He would stop every now and then to listen when there was the least noise below: and when he had satisfied himself, he would go on, whistling and stirring again, as before.

Although Oliver had roused himself from sleep, he was not thoroughly awake. There is a drowsy state, between sleeping and walking, when you dream more in five minutes with your eyes half open, and yourself half conscious of everything that is passing around you, than you would in five nights with your eyes fast closed, and your senses wrapt in perfect unconsciousness. At such times, a mortal knows just enough of what his mind is doing, to form some glimmering conception of its mighty powers, its bounding from earth and spurning time and space, when freed from the restraint of its corporeal associate.

Oliver was precisely in this condition. He saw the Jew with his half-closed eyes; heard his low whistling; and recognised the sound of the spoon grating against the saucepan's sides; and yet the self-same senses were mentally engaged, at the same time, in busy action with almost everybody he had ever known.

When the coffee was done, the Jew drew the saucepan to the hob. Standing, then, in an irresolute attitude for a few minutes, as if he did not well know how to employ himself, he turned round and looked at Oliver, and called him by his name. He did not answer, and was to all appearance asleep.

After satisfying himself upon this head, the Jew stepped gently to the door: which he fastened. He then drew forth: as it seemed to Oliver, from some trap in the floor: a small box, which he placed carefully on the table. His eyes glistened as he raised the lid, and looked in. Dragging an old chair to the table, he sat down; and took from it a magnificent gold watch, sparkling with jewels.

"Aha!" said the Jew, shrugging up his shoulders, and distorting every feature with a hideous grin. "Clever dogs! Clever dogs! Staunch to the last! Never told the old parson where they were. Never peached upon old Fagin! And why should they? It wouldn't have loosened the knot, or kept the drop up, a minute longer. No, no, no! Fine fellows! Fine fellows!"

With these, and other muttered reflections of the like nature, the Jew once more deposited the watch in its place of safety. At least half a dozen more were severally drawn forth from the same box, and surveyed with equal pleasure; besides rings, brooches, bracelets, and other articles of jewellery, of such magnificent materials, and costly workmanship, that Oliver had no idea, even of their names.

Having replaced these trinkets, the Jew took out another: so small that it lay in the palm of his hand. There seemed to be some very minute inscription on it; for the Jew laid it flat upon the table, and, shading it with his hand, pored over it, long and earnestly. At length he put it down, as if despairing of success; and, leaning back in his chair, muttered:

"What a fine thing capital punishment is! Dead men never repent; dead men never bring awkward stories to light. Ah, it's a fine thing for the trade! Five of 'em strung up in a row, and none left to play booty, or turn white-livered!"

As the Jew uttered these words, his bright dark eyes, which had been staring vacantly before him, fell on Oliver's face; the

SIMON VAN BOOY

boy's eyes were fixed on his in mute curiosity; and although the recognition was only for an instant—for the briefest space of time that can possibly be conceived—it was enough to show the old man that he had been observed. He closed the lid of the box with a loud crash; and, laying his hand on a bread knife which was on the table, started furiously up. He trembled very much though; for, even in his terror, Oliver could see that the knife quivered in the air.

"What's that?" said the Jew. "What do you watch me for? Why are you awake? What have you seen? Speak out, boy! Quick—quick! for your life!"

"I wasn't able to sleep any longer, sir," replied Oliver, meekly. "I am very sorry if I have disturbed you, sir."

"You were not awake an hour ago?" said the Jew, scowling fiercely on the boy.

"No! No, indeed!" replied Oliver.

"Are you sure?" cried the Jew; with a still fiercer look than before: and a threatening attitude.

"Upon my word I was not, sir," replied Oliver, earnestly. "I was not, indeed, sir."

"Tush, tush, my dear!" said the Jew, abruptly resuming his old manner, and playing with the knife a little, before he laid it down; as if to induce the belief that he had caught it up, in mere sport. "Of course I know that, my dear. I only tried to frighten you. You're a brave boy. Ha!

ha! you're a brave boy, Oliver." The Jew rubbed his hands with a chuckle, but glanced uneasily at the box, notwithstanding.

"Did you see any of these pretty things, my dear?" said the Jew, laying his hand upon it after a short pause.

"Yes, sir," replied Oliver.

"Ah!" said the Jew, turning rather pale. "They—they're mine, Oliver; my little property. All I have to live upon, in my old age. The folks call me a miser, my dear. Only a miser; that's all."

Oliver thought the old gentleman must be a decided miser to live in such a dirty place, with so many watches; but, thinking that perhaps his fondness for the Dodger and the other boys, cost him a good deal of money, he only cast a deferential look at the Jew, and asked if he might get up.

"Certainly, my dear, certainly," replied the old gentleman. "Stay. There's a pitcher of water in the corner by the door. Bring it here; and I'll give you a basin to wash in, my dear."

Oliver got up; walked across the room; and stooped for an instant to raise the pitcher. When he turned his head, the box was gone.

He had scarcely washed himself, and made everything tidy, by emptying the basin out of the window, agreeably to the Jew's directions, when the Dodger returned: accompanied by a very sprightly young friend, whom Oliver had seen smoking on the previous night, and who was now formally introduced to him as Charley Bates. The four sat down, to breakfast, on the coffee, and some hot rolls and ham which the Dodger had brought home in the crown of his hat.

"Well," said the Jew, glancing slyly at Oliver, and addressing himself to the Dodger, "I hope you've been at work this morning, my dears?"

"Hard," replied the Dodger.

"As Nails," added Charley Bates.

"Good boys, good boys!" said the Jew. "What have you got, Dodger?"

"A couple of pocket-books," replied that young gentleman.

"Lined?" inquired the Jew, with eagerness.

"Pretty well," replied the Dodger, producing two pocket-books; one green, and the other red.

"Not so heavy as they might be," said the Jew, after looking at the insides carefully; "but very neat and nicely made. Ingenious workman, ain't he, Oliver?"

"Very, indeed, sir," said Oliver. At which Mr. Charles Bates laughed uproariously; very much to the amazement of Oliver, who saw nothing to laugh at, in anything that had passed.

"And what have you got, my dear?" said Fagin to Charley Bates.

"Wipes," replied Master Bates; at the same time producing four pocket-handkerchiefs.

"Well," said the Jew, inspecting them closely; "they're very good ones, very. You haven't marked them well, though, Charley; so the marks shall be picked out with a needle, and we'll teach Oliver how to do it. Shall us, Oliver, eh? Ha! ha! ha!"

"If you please, sir," said Oliver.

"You'd like to be able to make pocket-handkerchiefs as easy as Charley Bates, wouldn't you, my dear?" said the Jew.

"Very much, indeed, if you'll teach me, sir," replied Oliver.

Master Bates saw something so exquisitely ludicrous in this reply that he burst into another laugh; which laugh, meeting the coffee he was drinking, and carrying it down some wrong channel, very nearly terminated in his premature suffocation.

"He is so jolly green!" said Charley when he recovered, as an apology to the company for his unpolite behaviour.

The Dodger said nothing, but he smoothed Oliver's hair over his eyes, and said he'd know better, by-and-by; upon which the old gentleman, observing Oliver's colour mounting, changed the subject by asking whether there had been much of a crowd at the execution that morning? This made him wonder more and more; for it was plain from the replies of the two boys that they had both been there; and Oliver naturally wondered how they could possibly have found time to be so very industrious.

When the breakfast was cleared away, the merry old gentleman and the two boys played at a very curious and uncommon game, which was performed in this way. The merry old gentleman, placing a snuff-box in one pocket of his trousers, a note-case in the other, and a watch in his waistcoat pocket, with a guard-chain round his neck, and sticking a mock diamond pin in his shirt: buttoned his coat tight round him, and putting his spectacle-case and handkerchief in his pockets, trotted up and down the room with a stick, in imitation of the manner in which old gentlemen walk about the streets any hour in the day. Sometimes he stopped at the fire-place, and sometimes at the door, making believe that he was staring with all his might into shop-windows. At such times he would look constantly round him, for fear of thieves, and would keep slapping all his pockets in turn, to see that he hadn't lost anything, in such a very funny and natural manner, that Oliver laughed till the tears ran down his face. All this time, the two boys followed him closely about: getting out of his sight, so nimbly, every time he turned round, that it was impossible to follow their motions. At last, the Dodger trod upon his toes, or ran upon his boot accidentally, while Charley Bates stumbled up against him behind; and in that one moment they took from him, with the most extraordinary rapidity, snuff-box, note-case, watch-guard, chain, shirt-pin, pocket-handkerchief, even the spectacle-case. If the old gentleman felt a hand in any one of his pockets, he cried out where it was; and then the game began all over again.

When this game had been played a great many times, a couple of young ladies called to see the young gentlemen; one of whom was named Bet, and the other Nancy. They wore a good deal of hair, not very neatly turned up behind, and were rather untidy about the shoes and stockings. They were not exactly pretty, perhaps; but they had a great deal of colour in their faces, and looked quite stout and hearty. Being remarkably free and agreeable in their manners, Oliver thought them very nice girls indeed. As there is no doubt they were.

These visitors stopped a long time. Spirits were produced, in consequence of one of the young ladies complaining of a coldness in her inside; and the conversation took a very convivial and improving turn. At length, Charley Bates expressed his opinion that it was time to pad the hoof. This, it occurred to Oliver, must be French for going out; for, directly afterwards, the Dodger, and Charley, and the two young ladies, went away together, having been kindly furnished by the amiable old Jew with money to spend.

"There, my dear," said Fagin. "That's a pleasant life, isn't it? They have gone out for the day."

"Have they done work, sir?" inquired Oliver.

"Yes," said the Jew; "that is, unless they should unexpectedly come across any, when they are out; and they won't neglect it, if they do, my dear, depend upon it. Make 'em your models, my dear. Make 'em your models," tapping the fire-shovel on the hearth to add force to his words; "do everything they bid you, and take their advice in all matters—especially the Dodger's, my dear. He'll be a great man himself, and will make you one too, if you take pattern by him—Is my handkerchief hanging out of my pocket, my dear?" said the Jew, stopping short.

"Yes, sir," said Oliver.

"See if you can take it out, without my feeling it: as you saw them do, when we were at play this morning."

Oliver held up the bottom of the pocket with one hand, as he had seen the Dodger hold it, and drew the handkerchief lightly out of it with the other.

"Is it gone?" cried the Jew.

"Here it is, sir," said Oliver, showing it in his hand.

"You're a clever boy, my dear," said the playful old gentleman, patting Oliver on the head approvingly. "I never saw a sharper lad. Here's a shilling for you. If you go on, in this way, you'll be the greatest man of the time. And now come here, and I'll show you how to take the marks out of the handkerchiefs."

Oliver wondered what picking the old gentleman's pocket in play, had to do with his chances of being a great man. But, thinking that the Jew, being so much his senior, must know best, he followed him quietly to the table, and was soon deeply involved in his new study.

SON

Was my father a traitor, mother?

LADY MACDUFF

Ay, that he was.

SON

What is a traitor?

LADY MACDUFF

Why, one that swears and lies.

SON

And be all traitors that do so?

LADY MACDUFF

Every one that does so is a traitor, and must be hanged.

SON

And must they all be hanged that swear and lie?

LADY MACDUFF

Every one.

SON

Who must hang them?

LADY MACDUFF

Why, the honest men.

SON

Then the liars and swearers are fools,

for there are liars and swearers enow to beat

the honest men, and hang up them.

—William Shakespeare from Macbeth

Walt Whitman is one of America's most loved poets. He lived in the nineteenth century and taught himself by visiting museums and libraries. By fourteen he was living alone in Brooklyn and working full-time.

He is most famous for his self-published book, *Leaves of Grass*. In his time, Whitman's poems caused quite a stir—not only because he abandoned meter and rhyme in favor of free verse, but because he was outspoken on issues such as war, racism, slavery, sexuality, patriotism, human rights, and democracy.

In the opening lines of *Leaves of Grass*, Whitman suggests that a child's environment can influence who that child becomes.

Walt Whitman

from "There Was a Child Went Forth"

There was a child went forth every day.

And the first object he look'd upon, that object he became,

And that object became part of him for the day or a certain
    part of the day,

Or for many years or stretching cycles of years.

Emily Brontë spent her childhood creating imaginary worlds and playing in the wild, rain-swept moorland around her home in Haworth, England. Her mother died when she was three and her two oldest sisters died when she was seven. Emily Brontë's one and only novel, *Wuthering Heights*, was published under a pseudonym, Ellis Bell, when she was twenty-nine. She died a year later from tuberculosis.

In *Wuthering Heights*, Brontë tells the story of Heathcliff, a homeless orphan rescued from the streets of Victorian Liverpool.

Emily Brontë

from *Wuthering Heights*

One fine summer morning—it was the beginning of harvest. I remember—Mr. Earnshaw, the old master, came downstairs, dressed for a journey; and, after he had told Joseph what was to be done during the day, he turned to Hindley, and Cathy, and me—for I sat eating my porridge with them—and he said, speaking to his son—

"Now, my bonny man, I'm going to Liverpool, today. What shall I bring you? You may choose what you like; only let it be little, for I shall walk there and back; sixty miles each way, that is a long spell!"

Hindley named a fiddle, and then he asked Miss Cathy; she was hardly six years old, but she could ride any horse in the stable, and she chose a whip.

He did not forget me, for he had a kind heart, though he was rather severe, sometimes. He promised to bring me a pocketful of apples and pears, and then he kissed his children good-bye, and set off.

It seemed a long while to us all—the three days of his absence—and often did little Cathy ask when he would be home. Mrs. Earnshaw expected him by supper-time, on the third evening; and she put the meal off hour after hour; there were no signs of his coming, however, and at last the children got tired of running down to the gate to look. Then it grew dark; she would have had them to bed, but they begged sadly to be allowed to stay up; and, just about eleven o'clock, the door-latch was raised quietly and in stept the master. He threw himself into a chair, laughing and groaning, and bid them all stand off, for he was nearly killed—he would not have such another walk for the three kingdoms.

"And at the end of it, to be flighted to death!" he said, opening his great-coat, which he held bundled up in his arms. "See here, wife; I was never so beaten with anything in my life; but you must e'en take it as a gift of God, though it's as dark almost as if it came from the devil."

We crowded round, and, over Miss Cathy's head, I had a peep at a dirty, ragged, black-haired child; big enough both to walk and talk—indeed, its face looked older than Catherine's—yet, when it was set on its feet, it only stared round, and repeated over and over again some gibberish that nobody could understand. I was frightened, and Mrs. Earnshaw was ready to fling it out of doors; she did fly up—asking how he could fashion to bring that gipsy brat into the house, when they had their own bairns to feed and fend for? What he meant to do with it, and whether he were mad?

The master tried to explain the matter; but he was really half dead with fatigue, and all that I could make out, amongst her scolding, was a tale of his seeing it starving, and houseless, and as good as dumb in the streets of Liverpool, where he picked it up and inquired for its owner. Not a soul knew to whom it belonged, he said . . . and his money and time being both limited, he thought it better to take it home with him at once, than run into vain expenses there; because he was determined he would not leave it as he found it.

Well, the conclusion was that my mistress grumbled herself calm; and Mr. Earnshaw told me to wash it, and give it clean things, and let it sleep with the children.

Hindley and Cathy contented themselves with looking and listening till peace was restored; then, both began searching their father's pockets for the presents he had promised them. The former was a boy of fourteen, but when he drew out what had been a fiddle, crushed to morsels in the great-coat, he blubbered aloud, and Cathy, when she learnt the master had lost her whip in attending on the stranger, showed her humour by grinning and spitting at the stupid little thing, earning for her pains a sound blow from her father to teach her cleaner manners.

They entirely refused to have it in bed with them, or even in their room, and I had no more sense, so I put it on the landing of the stairs, hoping it might be gone on the morrow. By chance, or else attracted by hearing his voice, it crept to Mr. Earnshaw's door and there he found it on quitting his chamber. Inquiries were made as to how it got there; I was obliged to confess, and in recompense for my cowardice and inhumanity was sent out of the house.

This was Heathcliff's first introduction to the family. On coming back a few days afterwards, for I did not consider my banishment perpetual, I found they had christened him "Heathcliff"; it was the name of a son who died in childhood, and it has served him ever since, both for Christian and surname.

Miss Cathy and he were now very thick; but Hindley hated him, and to say the truth I did the same; and we plagued and went on with him shamefully, for I wasn't reasonable enough to feel my injustice, and the mistress never put in a word on his behalf when she saw him wronged.

He seemed a sullen, patient child, hardened, perhaps, to ill-treatment: he would stand Hindley's blows without winking or shedding a tear, and my pinches moved him only to draw in a breath, and open his eyes as if he had hurt himself by accident, and nobody was to blame.

This endurance made old Earnshaw furious when he discovered his son persecuting the poor, fatherless child, as he called him. He took to Heathcliff strangely, believing all he said (for that matter, he said precious little, and generally the truth) and petting him up far above Cathy, who was too mischievous and wayward for a favourite.

So, from the very beginning, he bred bad feeling in the house; and at Mrs. Earnshaw's death, which happened in less than two years after, the young master had learnt to regard his father as an oppressor rather than a friend, and Heathcliff

SIMON VAN BOOY

as a usurper of his parent's affections and his privileges, and he grew bitter with brooding over these injuries.

I sympathised a while, but, when the children fell ill of the measles and I had to tend them, and take on me the cares of a woman at once, I changed my ideas. Heathcliff was dangerously sick, and while he lay at the worst he would have me constantly by his pillow. I suppose he felt I did a good deal for him, and he hadn't wit to guess that I was compelled to do it. However, I will say this, he was the quietest child that ever nurse watched over. The difference between him and the others forced me to be less partial. Cathy and her brother harassed me terribly; *he* was as uncomplaining as a lamb, though hardness, not gentleness, made him give little trouble.

He got through, and the doctor affirmed it was in a great measure owing to me, and praised me for my care. I was vain of his commendations, and softened towards the being by whose means I earned them, and thus Hindley lost his last ally; still I couldn't dote on Heathcliff, and I wondered often what my master saw to admire so much in the sullen boy who never, to my recollection, repaid his indulgence by any sign of gratitude. He was not insolent to his benefactor; he was simply insensible, though knowing perfectly the hold he had on his heart, and conscious he had only to speak and all the house would be obliged to bend to his wishes.

As an instance, I remember Mr. Earnshaw once bought a couple of colts at the parish fair, and gave the lads each one. Heathcliff took the handsomest, but it soon fell lame, and when he discovered it, he said to Hindley—

"You must exchange horses with me; I don't like mine, and if you won't I shall tell your father of the three thrashings you've given me this week, and show him my arm, which is black to the shoulder."

Hindley put out his tongue, and cuffed him over the ears.

"You'd better do it at once," he persisted, escaping to the porch (they were in the stable); "you will have to, and if I speak of these blows, you'll get them again with interest."

"Off, dog!" cried Hindley, threatening him with an iron weight, used for weighing potatoes and hay.

"Throw it," he replied, standing still, "and then I'll tell how you boasted that you would turn me out of doors as soon as he died and see whether he will not turn you out directly."

Hindley threw it, hitting him on the breast, and down he fell, but staggered up immediately, breathless and white, and had not I prevented it he would have gone just so to the master, and got full revenge by letting his condition plead for him, intimating who had caused it.

"Take my colt, gipsy, then!" said young Earnshaw. "And I pray that he may break your neck; take him, and be damned, you beggarly interloper! and wheedle my father out of all he

has, only afterwards show him what you are, imp of Satan—
And take that, I hope he'll kick out your brains!"

Heathcliff had gone to loose the beast, and shift it to his own stall. He was passing behind it, when Hindley finished his speech by knocking him under its feet, and without stopping to examine whether his hopes were fulfilled, ran away as fast as he could.

I was surprised to witness how coolly the child gathered himself up, and went on with his intention, exchanging saddles and all, and then sitting down on a bundle of hay to overcome the qualm which the violent blow occasioned, before he entered the house.

I persuaded him easily to let me lay the blame of his bruises on the horse; he minded little what tale was told since he had what he wanted. He complained so seldom, indeed, of such stirs as these, that I really thought him not vindictive—I was deceived completely, as you will hear.

CHAPTER V

In the course of time, Mr. Earnshaw began to fail. He had been active and healthy, yet his strength left him suddenly; and when he was confined to the chimney-corner he grew grievously irritable. A nothing vexed him, and suspected slights of his authority nearly threw him into fits.

This was especially to be remarked if any one attempted to impose upon, or domineer over, his favourite: he was painfully jealous lest a word should be spoken amiss to him, seeming to have got into his head the notion that, because he liked Heathcliff, all hated, and longed to do him an ill-turn.

It was a disadvantage to the lad, for the kinder among us did not wish to fret the master, so we humoured his partiality; and that humouring was rich nourishment to the child's pride and black tempers. Still it became in a manner necessary; twice, or thrice, Hindley's manifestations of scorn, while his father was near, roused the old man to a fury. He seized his stick to strike him, and shook with rage that he could not do it.

At last, our curate (we had a curate then who made the living answer by teaching the little Lintons and Earnshaws, and farming his bit of land himself)—he advised that the young man should be sent to college, and Mr. Earnshaw agreed, though with a heavy spirit, for he said—

"Hindley was naught, and would never thrive as where he wandered."

I hoped heartily we should have peace now. It hurt me to think the master should be made uncomfortable by his own good deed. I fancied the discontent of age and disease arose from his family disagreements, as he would have it that it did; really, you know, sir, it was in his sinking frame.

We might have got on tolerably, notwithstanding, but for two people. Miss Cathy and Joseph, the servant; you saw him, I dare say, up yonder. He was, and is yet, most likely, the wearisomest, self-righteous pharisee that ever ransacked a Bible to rake the promises to himself, and fling the curses on his neighbours. By his knack of sermonizing and pious discoursing, he contrived to make a great impression on Mr. Earnshaw, and the more feeble the master became, the more influence he gained.

He was relentless in worrying him about his soul's concerns, and about ruling his children rigidly. He encouraged him to regard Hindley as a reprobate; and, night after night, he regularly grumbled out a long string of tales against Heathcliff and Catherine; always minding to flatter Earnshaw's weakness by heaping the heaviest blame on the last.

Certainly, she had ways with her such as I never saw a child take up before; and she put all of us past our patience fifty times and oftener in a day: from the hour she came downstairs, till the hour she went to bed, we had not a minute's security that she wouldn't be in mischief. Her spirits were always at high-water mark, her tongue always going—singing, laughing, and plaguing everybody who would not do the same. A wild, wick slip she was—but she had the bonniest eye, and sweetest smile, and lightest foot in the parish; and, after all, I believe she meant no harm; for when once she made you cry in good earnest, it seldom happened that she would not keep you company, and oblige you to be quiet that you might comfort her.

She was much too fond of Heathcliff. The greatest punishment we could invent for her was to keep her separate from him: yet she got chided more than any of us on his account.

In play, she liked, exceedingly, to act the little mistress; using her hands freely, and commanding her companions: she did so to me, but I would not bear slapping and ordering, and so I let her know.

Now, Mr. Earnshaw did not understand jokes from his children: he had always been strict and grave with them; and Catherine, on her part, had no idea why her father should be crosser and less patient in his ailing condition, than he was in his prime.

His peevish reproofs wakened in her a naughty delight to provoke him; she was never so happy as when we were all scolding her at once, and she defying us with her bold, saucy look, and her ready words; turning Joseph's religious curses into ridicule, baiting me, and doing just what her father hated most, showing how her pretended insolence, which he thought real, had more power over Heathcliff than his kindness; how the boy would do *her* bidding in anything, and *his* only when it suited his own inclination.

After behaving as badly as possible all day, she sometimes came fondling to make it up at night.

"Nay, Cathy," the old man would say, "I cannot love thee; thou'rt worse than thy brother. Go, say thy prayers, child, and ask God's pardon. I doubt thy mother and I must rue that we ever reared thee!"

That made her cry, at first; and then, being repulsed continually hardened her, and she laughed if I told her to say she was sorry for her faults, and beg to be forgiven.

But the hour came, at last, that ended Mr. Earnshaw's troubles on earth. He died quietly in his chair one October evening, seated by the fire-side.

A high wind blustered round the house, and roared in the chimney: it sounded wild and stormy, yet it was not cold, and we were all together—I, a little removed from the hearth, busy at my knitting, and Joseph reading his Bible near the table (for the servants generally sat in the house then, after their work was done). Miss Cathy had been sick, and that made her still; she leant against her father's knee, and Heathcliff was lying on the floor with his head in her lap.

I remember the master, before he fell into a doze, stroking her bonny hair—it pleased him rarely to see her gentle—and saying—

"Why canst thou not always be a good lass, Cathy?"

And she turned her face up to his, and laughed, and answered—

"Why cannot you always be a good man, father?"

WHY WE FIGHT

But as soon as she saw him vexed again, she kissed his hand, and said she would sing him to sleep. She began singing very low, till his fingers dropped from hers, and his head sank on his breast. Then I told her to hush, and not stir, for fear she should wake him. We all kept as mute as mice a full half-hour, and should have done so longer, only Joseph, having finished his chapter, got up and said that he must rouse the master for prayers and bed. He stepped forward, and called him by name, and touched his shoulder, but he would not move—so he took the candle and looked at him.

I thought there was something wrong as he set down the light; and seizing the children each by an arm, whispered them to "frame upstairs, and make little din—they might pray alone that evening—he had summut to do."

"I shall bid father good-night first," said Catherine, putting her arms round his neck, before we could hinder her.

The poor thing discovered her loss directly—she screamed out—

"Oh, he's dead, Heathcliff! he's dead!"

And they both set up a heart-breaking cry.

I joined my wail to theirs, loud and bitter; but Joseph asked what we could be thinking of to roar in that way over a saint in heaven. *

He told me to put on my cloak and run to Gimmerton for the doctor and the parson. I could not guess the use that either would be of, then. However, I went, through wind and rain, and brought one, the doctor, back with me; the other said he would come in the morning.

Leaving Joseph to explain matters, I ran to the children's room; their door was ajar. I saw they had never laid down, though it was past midnight; but they were calmer, and did not need me to console them. The little souls were comforting each other with better thoughts than I could have hit on; no parson in the world ever pictured heaven so beautifully as they did, in their innocent talk; and, while I sobbed and listened, I could not help wishing we were all there safe together.

On a mellow evening in September, I was coming from the garden with a heavy basket of apples which I had been gathering. It had got dusk, and the moon looked over the high wall of the court, causing undefined shadows to lurk in the corners of the numerous projecting portions of the building. I set my burden on the house steps by the kitchen door, and lingered to rest and draw in a few more breaths of the soft, sweet air; my eyes were on the moon, and my back to the entrance, when I heard a voice behind me say—

"Nelly, is that you?"

It was a deep voice, and foreign in tone; yet there was something in the manner of pronouncing my name which made it sound familiar. I turned about to discover who spoke, fearfully, for the doors were shut, and I had seen nobody on approaching the steps.

Something stirred in the porch; and moving nearer, I distinguished a tall man dressed in dark clothes, with dark face and hair. He leant against the side, and held his fingers on the latch, as if intending to open for himself.

"Who can it be?" I thought. "Mr. Earnshaw? Oh, no! The voice has no resemblance to his."

"I have waited here an hour," he resumed, while I continued staring; "and the whole of that time all round has been as still as death. I dared not enter. You do not know me? Look, I'm not a stranger!"

A ray fell on his features; the cheeks were sallow, and half covered with black whiskers; the brows lowering, the eyes deep set and singular. I remembered the eyes.

"What!" I cried, uncertain whether to regard him as a worldly visitor, and I raised my hands in amazement. "What! you come back? Is it really you? Is it?"

"Yes, Heathcliff," he replied, glancing from me up to the windows, which reflected a score of glittering moons, but showed no lights from within. "Are they at home—where is she? Nelly, you are not glad—you needn't be so disturbed. Is she here? Speak! I want to have one word with her—your mistress. Go, and say some person from Gimmerton desires to see her."

"How will she take it?" I exclaimed. "What will she do? The surprise bewilders me—it will put her out of her head! And you *are* Heathcliff? But altered! Nay, there's no comprehending it. Have you been for a soldier?"

"Go, and carry my message," he interrupted impatiently; "I'm in hell till you do!"

He lifted the latch, and I entered; but when I got to the parlour where Mr. and Mrs. Linton were, I could not persuade myself to proceed.

At length, I resolved on making an excuse to ask if they would have the candles lighted, and I opened the door.

They sat together in a window whose lattice lay back against the wall, and displayed, beyond the garden trees and the wild green park, the valley of Gimmerton, with a long line of mist winding nearly to its top (for very soon after you pass the chapel, as you may have noticed, the sough that runs from the marshes joins a beck which follows the bend of the glen). Wuthering Heights rose above this silvery vapour; but our old house was invisible—it rather dips down on the other side.

Both the room and its occupants, and the scene they gazed on, looked wondrously peaceful. I shrank reluctantly from performing my errand, and was actually going away, leaving it unsaid, after having put my question about the candles, when a sense of my folly compelled me to return, and mutter—

"A person from Gimmerton wishes to see you, ma'am."

"What does he want?" asked Mrs. Linton.

"I did not question him," I answered.

"Well, close the curtains, Nelly," she said; "and bring up tea. I'll be back again directly."

She quitted the apartment; Mr. Edgar inquired carelessly, who it was?

"Some one the mistress does not expect," I replied. "That Heathcliff, you recollect him, sir, who used to live at Mr. Earnshaw's."

"What, the gipsy—the ploughboy?" he cried. "Why did you not say so to Catherine?"

"Hush! you must not call him by those names, master," I said. "She'd be sadly grieved to hear you. She was nearly heart-broken when he ran off; I guess his return will make a jubilee to her."

Mr. Linton walked to a window on the other side of the room that overlooked the court. He unfastened it, and leant out. I suppose they were below, for he exclaimed, quickly—

"Don't stand there, love! Bring the person in, if it be any one particular."

Ere long, I heard the click of the latch, and Catherine flew upstairs, breathless and wild, too excited to show gladness; indeed, by her face, you would rather have surmised an awful calamity.

"Oh, Edgar, Edgar!" she panted, flinging her arms round his

neck. "Oh, Edgar, darling! Heathcliff's come back—he is!" And she tightened her embrace to a squeeze.

"Well, well," cried her husband, crossly, "don't strangle me for that! He never struck me as such a marvellous treasure. There is no need to be frantic!"

"I know you didn't like him," she answered, repressing a little the intensity of her delight. "Yet, for my sake, you must be friends now. Shall I tell him to come up?"

"Here?" he said, "into the parlour?"

"Where else?" she asked.

He looked vexed, and suggested the kitchen as a more suitable place for him.

Mrs. Linton eyed him with a droll expression—half angry, half laughing at his fastidiousness.

"No," she added, after a while; "I cannot sit in the kitchen. Set two tables here, Ellen; one for your master and Miss Isabella, being gentry; the other for Heathcliff and myself, being of the lower orders. Will that please you, dear? Or must I have a fire lighted elsewhere? If so, give directions. I'll run down and secure my guest. I'm afraid the joy is too great to be real!"

She was about to dart off again; but Edgar arrested her.

"*You* bid him step up," he said, addressing me; "and, Catherine, try to be glad, without being absurd! The whole household need not witness the sight of your welcoming a runaway servant as a brother."

I descended and found Heathcliff waiting under the porch, evidently anticipating an invitation to enter. He followed my guidance without waste of words, and I ushered him into the presence of the master and mistress, whose flushed cheeks betrayed signs of warm talking. But the lady's glowed with another feeling when her friend appeared at the door; she sprang forward, took both his hands, and led him to Linton; and then she seized Linton's reluctant fingers and crushed them into his.

Now fully revealed by the fire and candlelight. I was amazed, more than ever, to behold the transformation of Heathcliff. He had grown a tall, athletic, well-formed man, beside whom my master seemed quite slender and youth-like. His upright carriage suggested the idea of his having been in the army. His countenance was much older in expression and decision of feature than Mr. Linton's; it looked intelligent, and retained no marks of former degradation. A half-civilized ferocity lurked yet in the depressed brows and eyes full of black fire, but it was subdued; and his manner was even dignified, quite divested of roughness, though too stern for grace.

My master's surprise equalled or exceeded mine: he remained for a minute at a loss how to address the ploughboy, as he had called him. Heathcliff dropped his slight hand, and stood looking at him coolly till he chose to speak.

"Sit down, sir," he said, at length. "Mrs. Linton, recalling old times, would have me give you a cordial reception, and, of course, I am gratified when anything occurs to please her."

"And I also," answered Heathcliff, "especially if it be anything in which I have a part. I shall stay an hour or two willingly."

He took a seat opposite Catherine, who kept her gaze fixed on him as if she feared he would vanish were she to remove it. He did not raise his to her often, a quick glance now and then sufficed; but it flashed back, each time more confidently the undisguised delight he drank from hers.

They were too much absorbed in their mutual joy to suffer embarrassment. Not so Mr. Edgar; he grew pale with pure annoyance, a feeling that reached its climax when his lady rose, and stepping across the rug, seized Heathcliff's hands again, and laughed like one beside herself.

"I shall think it a dream tomorrow!" she cried. "I shall not be able to believe that I have seen, and touched, and spoken to you once more—and yet, cruel Heathcliff! you don't deserve this welcome. To be absent and silent for three years, and never to think of me!"

"A little more than you have thought of me!" he murmured. "I heard of your marriage, Cathy, not long since, and, while waiting in the yard below, I meditated this plan: just to have one glimpse of your face, a stare of surprise, perhaps, and pretended pleasure; afterwards settle my score with Hindley; and then prevent the law by doing execution on myself. Your welcome has put these ideas out of my mind; but beware of meeting me with another aspect next time! Nay, you'll not drive me off again. You were really sorry for me, were you? Well, there was cause. I've fought through a bitter life since I last heard your voice, and you must forgive me, for I struggled only for you."

SIMON VAN BOOY

Carl Julius von Leypold, *Wanderer in the Storm,* 1835

No matter how much cats fight, there always seem to be plenty of kittens.

—*Abraham Lincoln*

In 1882 James Joyce was born in Ireland, "one of sixteen or seventeen children" according to his father (the eldest of ten in real life), he lived most of his life in self-imposed exile in Zurich and Paris—where he scraped a living together teaching English. Joyce also relied on the generosity of friends and patrons who believed in his work and supported him wholeheartedly.

In the summer of 1904, when Joyce was twenty-two, he met a girl named Nora Barnacle, a chambermaid at Finn's Hotel in Dublin. They had two children and were to remain together until Joyce's death in 1941.

Joyce's literary life was not easy, and his attempts to publish were often fraught with struggle and legal intervention. In 1922, five hundred copies of *Ulysses* were burned by the U.S. Department of the Post Office. Many scholars believe that the publication of Joyce's *Ulysses* changed the course of Western literature.

In the story "Counterparts" (from *Dubliners*), the central character fights to express the anger of unresolved conflict, transferring aggression onto his young, defenseless child.

James Joyce

"Counterparts" from *Dubliners*

The bell rang furiously and, when Miss Parker went to the tube, af furious voice called out in a piercing North of Ireland accent:

—Send Farrington here!

Miss Parker returned to her machine, saying to a man who was writing at a desk:

—Mr Alleyne wants you upstairs.

The man muttered *Blast him!* under his breath and pushed back his chair to stand up. When he stood up he was tall and of great bulk. He had a hanging face, dark wine-coloured, with fair eyebrows and moustache: his eyes bulged forward slightly and the whites of them were dirty. He lifted up the counter and, passing by the clients, went out of the office with a heavy step.

He went heavily upstairs until he came to the second landing, where a door bore a brass plate with the inscription *Mr Alleyne*. Here he halted, puffing with labour and vexation, and knocked. The shrill voice cried:

—Come in! •

The man entered Mr Alleyne's room. Simultaneously Mr Alleyne, a little man wearing gold-rimmed glasses on a clean-shaven face, shot his head up over a pile of documents. The head itself was so pink and hairless that it seemed like a large egg reposing on the papers. Mr Alleyne did not lose a moment:

—Farrington? What is the meaning of this? Why have I always to complain of you? May I ask you why you haven't made a copy of that contract between Bodley and Kirwan? I told you it must be ready by four o'clock.

—But Mr Shelley said, sir—

—*Mr Shelley said, sir.* . . . Kindly attend to what I say and not to what *Mr Shelley says, sir.* You have always some excuse or another for shirking work. Let me tell you that if the contract is not copied before this evening I'll lay the matter before Mr Crosbie. . . . Do you hear me now?

—Yes, sir.

—Do you hear me now? . . . Ay and another little matter! I might as well be talking to the wall as talking to you. Understand once for all that you get a half an hour for your lunch and not an hour and a half. How many courses do you want, I'd like to know. . . . Do you mind me, now?

—Yes, sir.

Mr Alleyne bent his head again upon his pile of papers. The man stared fixedly at the polished skull which directed the affairs of Crosbie & Alleyne, gauging its fragility. A spasm of rage gripped his throat for a few moments and then passed, leaving after it a sharp sensation of thirst. The man recognised the sensation and felt that he must have a good night's drinking. The middle of the month was passed and, if he could get the copy done in time, Mr Alleyne might give him an order on the cashier. He stood still, gazing fixedly at the head upon the pile of papers. Suddenly Mr Alleyne began to upset all the papers, searching for something. Then, as if he had been unaware of the man's presence till that moment, he shot up his head again, saying:

—Eh? Are you going to stand there all day? Upon my word, Farrington, you take things easy!

—I was waiting to see . . .

—Very good, you needn't wait to see. Go downstairs and do your work.

The man walked heavily towards the door and, as he went out of the room, he heard Mr Alleyne cry after him that if the contract was not copied by evening Mr Crosbie would hear of the matter.

He returned to his desk in the lower office and counted the sheets which remained to be copied. He took up his pen and dipped it in the ink but he continued to stare stupidly at the last words he had written: *In no case shall the said Bernard Bodley be* . . . The evening was falling and in a few minutes they would be lighting the gas: then he could write. He felt that he must slake the thirst in his throat. He stood up from his desk and, lifting the counter as before, passed out of the office. As he was passing out the chief clerk looked at him inquiringly.

—It's all right, Mr Shelley, said the man, pointing with his finger to indicate the objective of his journey.

The chief clerk glanced at the hat-rack but, seeing the row complete, offered no remark. As soon as he was on the landing the man pulled a shepherd's plaid cap out of his pocket, put it on his head and ran quickly down the rickety stairs. From the street door he walked on furtively on the inner side of the path towards the corner and all at once dived into a doorway. He was now safe in the dark snug of O'Neill's shop, and, filling up the little window that looked into the bar with his inflamed face, the colour of dark wine or dark meat, he called out:

—Here, Pat, give us a g.p., like a good fellow.

The curate brought him a glass of plain porter. The man drank it at a gulp and asked for a caraway seed. He put his penny on the counter and, leaving the curate to grope for it in the gloom, retreated out of the snug as furtively as he had entered it.

Darkness, accompanied by a thick fog, was gaining upon the dusk of February and the lamps in Eustace Street had been lit. The man went up by the houses until he reached the door of the office, wondering whether he could finish his copy in time. On the stairs a moist pungent odour of per-

SIMON VAN BOOY

fumes saluted his nose: evidently Miss Delacour had come while he was out in O'Neill's. He crammed his cap back again into his pocket and reentered the office, assuming an air of absent-mindedness.

—Mr Alleyne has been calling for you, said the chief clerk severely. Where were you?

The man glanced at the two clients who were standing at the counter as if to intimate that their presence prevented him from answering. As the clients were both male the chief clerk allowed himself a laugh.

—I know that game, he said. Five times in one day is a little bit. . . . Well, you better look sharp and get a copy of our correspondence in the Delacour case for Mr Alleyne.

This address in the presence of the public, his run upstairs and the porter he had gulped down so hastily confused the man and, as he sat down at his desk to get what was required, he realised how hopeless was the task of finishing his copy of the contract before half past five. The dark damp night was coming and he longed to spend it in the bars, drinking with his friends amid the glare of gas and the clatter of glasses. He got out the Delacour correspondence and passed out of the office. He hoped Mr Alleyne would not discover that the last two letters were missing.

The moist pungent perfume lay all the way up to Mr Alleyne's room. Miss Delacour was a middle-aged woman of

Jewish appearance. Mr Alleyne was said to be sweet on her or on her money. She came to the office often and stayed a long time when she came. She was sitting beside his desk now in an aroma of perfumes, smoothing the handle of her umbrella and nodding the great black feather in her hat. Mr Alleyne had swivelled his chair round to face her and thrown his right foot jauntily upon his left knee. The man put the correspondence on the desk and bowed respectfully but neither Mr Alleyne nor Miss Delacour took any notice of his bow. Mr Alleyne tapped a finger on the correspondence and then flicked it towards him as if to say: *That's all right: you can go.*

The man returned to the lower office and sat down again at his desk. He stared intently at the incomplete phrase: *In no case shall the said Bernard Bodley be . . .* and thought how strange it was that the last three words began with the same letter. The chief clerk began to hurry Miss Parker, saying she would never have the letters typed in time for post. The man listened to the clicking of the machine for a few minutes and then set to work to finish his copy. But his head was not clear and his mind wandered away to the glare and rattle of the public-house. It was a night for hot punches. He struggled on with his copy, but when the clock struck five he had still fourteen pages to write. Blast it! He couldn't finish it in time. He longed to execrate aloud, to bring his fist down on something violently. He was so enraged that he wrote *Bernard Bernard* instead of *Bernard Bodley* and had to begin again on a clean sheet.

He felt strong enough to clear out the whole office single-handed. His body ached to do something, to rush out and revel in violence. All the indignities of his life enraged him. . . . Could he ask the cashier privately for an advance? No, the cashier was no good, no damn good: he wouldn't give an advance. . . . He knew where he would meet the boys: Leonard and O'Halloran and Nosey Flynn. The barometer of his emotional nature was set for a spell of riot.

His imagination had so abstracted him that his name was called twice before he answered. Mr Alleyne and Miss Delacour were standing outside the counter and all the clerks had turned round in anticipation of something. The man got up from his desk. Mr Alleyne began a tirade of abuse, saying that two letters were missing. The man answered that he knew nothing about them, that he had made a faithful copy. The tirade continued: it was so bitter and violent that the man could hardly restrain his fist from descending upon the head of the manikin before him.

—I know nothing about any other two letters, he said stupidly.

—*You—know—nothing.* Of course you know nothing, said Mr Alleyne. Tell me, he added, glancing first for approval to the lady beside him, do you take me for a fool? Do you think me an utter fool?

The man glanced from the lady's face to the little egg-shaped head and back again; and, almost before he was aware of it, his tongue had found a felicitous moment:

—I don't think, sir, he said, that that's a fair question to put to me.

There was a pause in the very breathing of the clerks. Everyone was astounded (the author of the witticism no less than his neighbours) and Miss Delacour, who was a stout amiable person, began to smile broadly. Mr Alleyne flushed to the hue of a wild rose and his mouth twitched with a dwarf's passion. He shook his fist in the man's face till it seemed to vibrate like the knob of some electric machine:

—You impertinent ruffian! You impertinent ruffian! I'll make short work of you! Wait till you see! You'll apologise to me for your impertinence or you'll quit the office instanter! You'll quit this, I'm telling you, or you'll apologise to me!

He stood in a doorway opposite the office watching to see if the cashier would come out alone. All the clerks passed out and finally the cashier came out with the chief clerk. It was no use trying to say a word to him when he was with the chief clerk. The man felt that his position was bad enough. He had been obliged to offer an abject apology to Mr Alleyne for his impertinence but he knew what a hornet's nest the office would be for him. He could remember the way in which Mr Alleyne had hounded little Peake out of the office in order to make room for his own nephew. He felt savage and thirsty and revengeful, annoyed with himself and with everyone else. Mr Alleyne would never give him an hour's rest; his life would be a hell to him. He had made a proper fool of himself this time. Could he not keep his tongue in his cheek? But they had never pulled together from the first, he and Mr Alleyne, ever since the day Mr Alleyne had overheard him mimicking his North of Ireland accent to amuse Higgins and Miss Parker: that had been the beginning of it. He might have tried Higgins for the money, but sure Higgins never had anything for himself. A man with two establishments to keep up, of course he couldn't. . . .

He felt his great body again aching for the comfort of the public-house. The fog had begun to chill him and he wondered could he touch Pat in O'Neill's. He could not touch him for more than a bob—and a bob was no use. Yet he must get money somewhere or other: he had spent his last penny for the g.p. and soon it would be too late for getting money anywhere. Suddenly, as he was fingering his watch-chain, he thought of Terry Kelly's pawn-office in Fleet Street. That was the dart! Why didn't he think of it sooner?

He went through the narrow alley of Temple Bar quickly, muttering to himself that they could all go to hell because he was going to have a good night of it. The clerk in Terry Kelly's said *A crown!* but the consignor held out for six shillings; and in the end the six shillings was allowed him literally. He came out of the pawn-office joyfully, making a little cylinder of the coins between his thumb and fingers. In Westmoreland Street the footpaths were crowded with young men and women returning from business and ragged urchins ran here and there yelling out the names of the evening editions. The man passed through the crowd, looking on the spectacle generally with proud satisfaction and staring masterfully at the office-girls. His head was full of the noises of tram-gongs and swishing trolleys and his nose already sniffed the curling fumes of punch. As he walked on he preconsidered the terms in which he would narrate the incident to the boys:

—So, I just looked at him—coolly, you know, and looked at her. Then I looked back at him again—taking my time, you know. *I don't think that that's a fair question to put to me*, says I.

Nosey Flynn was sitting up in his usual corner of Davy Byrne's and, when he heard the story, he stood Farrington a half-one, saying it was as smart a thing as ever he heard. Farrington stood a drink in his turn. After a while O'Halloran and Paddy Leonard came in and the story was repeated to them. O'Halloran stood tailors of malt, hot, all round and told the story of the retort he had made to the chief clerk when he was in Callan's of Fownes's Street; but, as the retort was after

SIMON VAN BOOY

the manner of the liberal shepherds in the eclogues, he had to admit that it was not so clever as Farrington's retort. At this Farrington told the boys to polish off that and have another.

Just as they were naming their poisons who should come in but Higgins! Of course he had to join in with the others. The men asked him to give his version of it, and he did so with great vivacity for the sight of five small hot whiskies was very exhilarating. Everyone roared laughing when he showed the way in which Mr Alleyne shook his fist in Farrington's face. Then he imitated Farrington, saying, *And here was my nabs, as cool as you please*, while Farrington looked at the company out of his heavy dirty eyes, smiling and at times drawing forth stray drops of liquor from his moustache with the aid of his lower lip.

When that round was over there was a pause. O'Halloran had money but neither of the other two seemed to have any; so the whole party left the shop somewhat regretfully. At the corner of Duke Street Higgins and Nosey Flynn bevelled off to the left while the other three turned back towards the city. Rain was drizzling down on the cold streets and, when they reached the Ballast Office, Farrington suggested the Scotch House. The bar was full of men and loud with the noise of tongues and glasses. The three men pushed past the whining match-sellers at the door and formed a little party at the corner of the counter. They began to exchange stories. Leonard introduced them to a young fellow named Weathers who was performing at the Tivoli as an acrobat and knock-about *artiste*. Farrington stood a drink all round. Weathers said he would take a small Irish and Apollinaris. Farrington, who had definite notions of what was what, asked the boys would they have an Apollinaris too; but the boys told Tim to make theirs hot. The talk became theatrical. O'Halloran stood a round and then Farrington stood another round, Weathers protesting that the hospitality was too Irish. He promised to get them in behind the scenes and introduce them to some nice girls. O'Halloran said that he and Leonard would go but that Farrington wouldn't go because he was a married man; and Farrington's heavy dirty eyes leered at the company in token that he understood he was being chaffed. Weathers made them all have just one little tincture at his expense and promised to meet them later on at Mulligan's in Poolbeg Street.

When the Scotch House closed they went round to Mulligan's. They went into the parlour at the back and O'Halloran ordered small hot specials all round. They were all beginning to feel mellow. Farrington was just standing another round when Weathers came back. Much to Farrington's relief he drank a glass of bitter this time. Funds were running low but they had enough to keep them going. Presently two young women with big hats and a young man in a check suit came in and sat at a table close by. Weathers saluted them and told the company that they were out of the Tivoli. Farrington's eyes wandered at every moment in the direction of one of the young women. There was something striking in her appearance. An immense scarf of peacock-blue muslin was wound round her hat and knotted in a great bow under her chin; and she wore bright yellow gloves, reaching to the elbow. Farrington gazed admiringly at the plump arm which she moved very often and with much grace; and when, after a little time, she answered his gaze he admired still more her large dark brown eyes. The oblique staring expression in them fascinated him. She glanced at him once or twice and, when the party was leaving the room, she brushed against his chair and said *O, pardon!* in a London accent. He watched her leave the room in the hope that she would look back at him, but he was disappointed. He cursed his want of money and cursed all the rounds he had stood, particularly all the whiskies and Apollinaris which he had stood to Weathers. If there was one thing that he hated it was a sponge. He was so angry that he lost count of the conversation of his friends.

When Paddy Leonard called him he found that they were talking about feats of strength. Weathers was showing his biceps muscle to the company and boasting so much that the other two had called on Farrington to uphold the national honour. Farrington pulled up his sleeve accordingly and showed his biceps muscle to the company. The two arms were examined and compared and finally it was agreed to have a trial of strength. The table was cleared and the two men rested their elbows on it, clasping hands. When Paddy Leonard said *Go!* each was to try to bring down the other's hand on to the table. Farrington looked very serious and determined.

The trial began. After about thirty seconds Weathers brought his opponent's hand slowly down on to the table. Farrington's dark wine-coloured face flushed darker still with anger and humiliation at having been defeated by such a stripling.

—You're not to put the weight of your body behind it. Play fair, he said.

—Who's not playing fair? said the other.

—Come on again. The two best out of three.

The trial began again. The veins stood out on Farrington's forehead, and the pallor of Weathers' complexion changed to peony. Their hands and arms trembled under the stress. After a long struggle Weathers again brought his opponent's hand slowly on to the table. There was a murmur of applause from the spectators. The curate, who was standing beside the table, nodded his red head towards the victor and said with loutish familiarity:

—Ah! that's the knack!

—What the hell do you know about it? said Farrington fiercely, turning on the man. What do you put in your gab for?

—Sh, sh! said O'Halloran, observing the violent expression of Farrington's face. Pony up, boys. We'll have just one little smahan more and then we'll be off.

A very sullen-faced man stood at the corner of O'Connell Bridge waiting for the little Sandymount tram to take him home. He was full of smouldering anger and revengefulness. He felt humiliated and discontented; he did not even feel drunk; and he had only twopence in his pocket. He cursed everything. He had done for himself in the office, pawned his watch, spent all his money; and he had not even got drunk. He began to feel thirsty again and he longed to be back again in the hot reeking public-house. He had lost his reputation as a strong man, having been defeated twice by a mere boy. His heart swelled with fury and, when he thought of the woman in the big hat who had brushed against him and said *Pardon!* his fury nearly choked him.

His tram let him down at Shelbourne Road and he steered his great body along in the shadow of the wall of the barracks. He loathed returning to his home. When he went in by the side-door he found the kitchen empty and the kitchen fire nearly out. He bawled upstairs:

—Ada! Ada!

His wife was a little sharp-faced woman who bullied her husband when he was sober and was bullied by him when he was drunk. They had five children. A little boy came running down the stairs.

—Who is that? said the man, peering through the darkness.

—Me, pa.

—Who are you? Charlie?

—No, pa. Tom.

—Where's your mother?

—She's out at the chapel.

—That's right. . . . Did she think of leaving any dinner for me?

—Yes, pa. I—

—Light the lamp. What do you mean by having the place in darkness? Are the other children in bed?

The man sat down heavily on one of the chairs while the little boy lit the lamp. He began to mimic his son's flat accent, saying half to himself: *At the chapel. At the chapel, if you please!* When the lamp was lit he banged his fist on the table and shouted:

—What's for my dinner?

—I'm going . . . to cook it, pa, said the little boy.

The man jumped up furiously and pointed to the fire.

—On that fire! You let the fire out! By God, I'll teach you to do that again!

He took a step to the door and seized the walking-stick which was standing behind it.

SIMON VAN BOOY

—I'll teach you to let the fire out! he said, rolling up his sleeve in order to give his arm free play.

The little boy cried *O, pa!* and ran whimpering round the table, but the man followed him and caught him by the coat. The little boy looked about him wildly but, seeing no way of escape, fell upon his knees.

—Now, you'll let the fire out the next time! said the man, striking at him viciously with the stick. Take that, you little whelp!

The boy uttered a squeal of pain as the stick cut his thigh. He clasped his hands together in the air and his voice shook with fright.

—O, pa! he cried. Don't beat me, pa! And I'll . . . I'll say a *Hail Mary* for you. . . . I'll say a *Hail Mary* for you, pa, if you don't beat me. . . . I'll say a *Hail Mary*. . . .

Force is all-conquering, but its victories are short-lived.

—*Abraham Lincoln*

Born in England in 1893, Wilfred Owen was one of the first poets to describe the realities of modern warfare, and aggressively challenged what he referred to as "The old Lie":

Dulce et decorum est
Pro patria mori.

This Latin expression comes from the Roman poet Horace and means that it is "sweet and proper to die for one's country."

Owen does not agree, and the voice of the poem reaches out hauntingly to the reader, who might naively believe, from a comfortable armchair, that all war is glamorous and noble. Owen was killed a week before the war ended. News of his death reached his mother as the town church bells rang for peace.

Wilfred Owen

"Dulce et Decorum Est"

Bent double, like old beggars under sacks,

Knock-kneed, coughing like hags, we cursed through sludge,

Till on the haunting flares we turned our backs

And towards our distant rest began to trudge.

Men marched asleep. Many had lost their boots

But limped on, blood-shod. All went lame; all blind;

Drunk with fatigue; deaf even to the hoots

Of tired, outstripped Five-Nines that dropped behind.

Gas! Gas! Quick, boys!—An ecstasy of fumbling,

Fitting the clumsy helmets just in time;

But someone still was yelling out and stumbling

And flound'ring like a man in fire or lime . . .

Dim, through the misty panes and thick green light,

As under a green sea, I saw him drowning.

In all my dreams, before my helpless sight,

He plunges at me, guttering, choking, drowning.

If in some smothering dreams you too could pace

Behind the wagon that we flung him in,

And watch the white eyes writhing in his face,

His hanging face, like a devil's sick of sin;
If you could hear, at every jolt, the blood
Come gargling from the froth-corrupted lungs,
Obscene as cancer, bitter as the cud
Of vile, incurable sores on innocent tongues,—
My friend, you would not tell with such high zest
To children ardent for some desperate glory,
The old Lie: *Dulce et decorum est*
Pro patria mori.

In war, truth is the first casualty.

—*Aeschylus*

George Smith Patton Jr. was born in California in 1885. Patton decided during childhood that his goal in life was to become a hero. He graduated from the U.S. Military Academy at West Point in 1909. In 1912, he represented the United States at the Stockholm Olympics in the first Modern Pentathlon. In 1917, Patton became the first member of the newly established U.S. Tank Corps. Along with British tankers, Patton and his men achieved victory at Cambrai, France, during the world's first major tank battle in 1917. When the United States entered World War II, Patton successfully commanded campaigns in North Africa and Sicily. When he was given command of the Third Army in France in 1944, Patton and his troops swept through Europe after the Battle of Normandy, covering six hundred miles across France, Belgium, Luxembourg, Germany, Austria, and Czechoslovakia. When the Third Army liberated the

Buchenwald concentration camp, Patton instituted a policy of making local German civilians tour the camps. By the time WWII was over, the Third Army had liberated or conquered 81,522 square miles of territory. General Patton died soon after in 1945, from injuries sustained in a car accident. He is buried in Hamm, Luxembourg, among the soldiers who died in the Battle of the Bulge.

George Smith Patton Jr.

Speech to the Third Army, June 5, 1944

Be seated. Men, this stuff that some sources sling around about America wanting out of this war, not wanting to fight, is a crock of bullshit. Americans love to fight, traditionally. All real Americans love the sting and clash of battle.

You are here today for three reasons. First, because you are here to defend your homes and your loved ones. Second, you are here for your own self respect, because you would not want to be anywhere else. Third, you are here because you are real men and all real men like to fight. When you, here, every one of you, were kids, you all admired the champion marble player, the fastest runner, the toughest boxer, the big league ball players, and the All-American football players. Americans love a winner. Americans will not tolerate a loser. Americans despise cowards. Americans play to win all of the time. I wouldn't give a hoot in hell for a man who lost and laughed. That's why Americans have never lost nor will ever lose a war; for the very idea of losing is hateful to an American.

You are not all going to die. Only two percent of you right here today would die in a major battle. Death must not be feared. Death, in time, comes to all men. Yes, every man is scared in his first battle. If he says he's not, he's a liar. Some men are cowards but they fight the same as the brave men or they get the hell slammed out of them watching men fight who are just as scared as they are. The real hero is the man who fights even though he is scared. Some men get over their fright in a minute under fire. For some, it takes an hour. For some, it takes days. But a real man will never let his fear of death overpower his honor, his sense of duty to his country, and his innate manhood. Battle is the most magnificent competition in which a human being can indulge. It brings out all that is best and it removes all that is base. Americans pride themselves on being He Men and they ARE He Men.

Remember that the enemy is just as frightened as you are, and probably more so. They are not supermen. All through your Army careers, you men have bitched about what you call "chicken shit drilling." That, like everything else in this Army, has a definite purpose. That purpose is alertness. Alertness must be bred into every soldier. I don't give a fuck for a man who's not always on his toes.

You men are veterans or you wouldn't be here. You are ready for what's to come. A man must be alert at all times if he expects to stay alive. If you're not alert, sometime, a German son-of-an-asshole-bitch is going to sneak up behind you and beat you to death with a sock full of shit! There are four hundred neatly marked graves somewhere in Sicily, all because one man went to sleep on the job. But they are German graves, because we caught the bastard asleep before they did.

An Army is a team. It lives, sleeps, eats, and fights as a team. This individual heroic stuff is pure horse shit. The bilious bastards who write that kind of stuff for the *Saturday Evening Post* don't know any more about real fighting under fire than they know about fucking! We have the finest food, the finest equipment, the best spirit, and the best men in the world. Why, by God, I actually pity those poor sons-of-bitches we're going up against. By God, I do. My men don't surrender, and I don't want to hear of any soldier under my command being captured unless he has been hit. Even if you are hit, you can still fight back. That's not just bullshit either. The kind of man that I want in my command is just like the lieutenant in Libya, who, with a Luger against his chest, jerked off his helmet, swept the gun aside with one hand, and busted the hell out of the Kraut with his helmet. Then he jumped on the gun and went out and killed another German before they knew what the hell was coming off. And, all of that time, this man had a bullet through a lung. There was a real man!

All of the real heroes are not storybook combat fighters, either. Every single man in this Army plays a vital role. Don't ever let up. Don't ever think that your job is unimportant. Every man has a job to do and he must do it. Every man is a vital link in the great chain. What if every truck driver suddenly decided that he didn't like the whine of those shells overhead, turned yellow, and jumped headlong into a ditch? The cowardly bastard could say, "Hell, they won't miss me, just one man in thousands." But, what if every man thought that way? Where in the hell would we be now? What would our country, our loved ones, our homes, even the world, be like? No, Goddamn it, Americans don't think like that. Every man does his job. Every man serves the whole. Every department, every unit, is important in the vast scheme of this war. The ordnance men are needed to supply the guns and machinery of war to keep us rolling. The Quartermaster is needed to bring up food and clothes because where we are going there isn't a hell of a lot to steal. Every last man on K.P. has a job to do, even the one who heats our water to keep us from getting the G.I. Shits.

Each man must not think only of himself, but also of his buddy fighting beside him. We don't want yellow cowards in this Army. They should be killed off like rats. If not, they will go home after this war and breed more cowards. The brave men will breed more brave men. Kill off the Goddamned cowards and we will have a nation of brave men. One of the bravest men that I ever saw was a fellow on top of a telegraph pole in the midst of a furious fire fight in Tunisia. I stopped and asked what the hell he was doing up there at a time like that. He answered, "Fixing the wire, Sir." I asked, "Isn't that a little unhealthy right about now?" He answered, "Yes, Sir, but the Goddamned wire has to be fixed." I asked, "Don't those planes strafing the road bother you?" And he answered, "No, Sir, but you sure as hell do!"

Now, there was a real man. A real soldier. There was a man who devoted all he had to his duty, no matter how seemingly insignificant his duty might appear at the time, no matter how great the odds. And you should have seen those trucks on the rode to Tunisia. Those drivers were magnificent. All day and all night they rolled over those son-of-a-bitching roads, never stopping, never faltering from their course, with shells bursting all around them all of the time. We got through on good old American guts.

Many of those men drove for over forty consecutive hours. These men weren't combat men, but they were soldiers with a job to do. They did it, and in one hell of a way they did it. They were part of a team. Without team effort, without them, the fight would have been lost. All of the links in the chain pulled together and the chain became unbreakable.

Don't forget, you men don't know that I'm here. No mention of that fact is to be made in any letters. The world is not supposed to know what the hell happened to me. I'm not supposed to be commanding this Army. I'm not even supposed to be here in England. Let the first bastards to find out be the Goddamned Germans. Someday I want to see them raise up on their piss-soaked hind legs and howl, "Jesus Christ, it's the Goddamned Third Army again and that son-of-a-fucking-bitch Patton. We want to get the hell over there." The quicker we clean up this Goddamned mess, the quicker we can take a little jaunt against the purple pissing Japs and clean out their nest, too. Before the Goddamned Marines get all of the credit.

Sure, we want to go home. We want this war over with. The quickest way to get it over with is to go get the bastards who started it. The quicker they are whipped, the quicker we can go home. The shortest way home is through Berlin and Tokyo. And when we get to Berlin, I am personally going to shoot that paper hanging son-of-a-bitch Hitler. Just like I'd shoot a snake!

When a man is lying in a shell hole, if he just stays there all day, a German will get to him eventually. The hell with that idea. The hell with taking it. My men don't dig foxholes. I don't want them to. Foxholes only slow up an offensive. Keep moving. And don't give the enemy time to dig one either. We'll win this war, but we'll win it only by fighting and by showing the Germans that we've got more guts than they have; or ever will have. We're not going to just shoot the sons-of-bitches, we're going to rip out their living God-damned guts and use them to grease the treads of our tanks. We're going to murder those lousy Hun cock suckers by the bushel-fucking-basket.

War is a bloody, killing business. You've got to spill their blood, or they will spill yours. Rip them up the belly. Shoot them in the guts. When shells are hitting all around you and you wipe the dirt off your face and realize that instead of dirt it's the blood and guts of what once was your best friend beside you, you'll know what to do! I don't want to get any messages saying, "I am holding my position." We are not holding a Goddamned thing. Let the Germans do that. We are advancing constantly and we are not interested in holding onto anything, except the enemy's balls. We are going to twist his balls and kick the living shit out of him all of the time. Our basic plan of operation is to advance and to keep on advancing regardless of whether we have to go over, under, or through the enemy. We are going to go through him like crap through a goose; like shit through a tin horn!

From time to time there will be some complaints that we are pushing our people too hard. I don't give a good Goddamn about such complaints. I believe in the old and sound rule that an ounce of sweat will save a gallon of blood. The harder WE push, the more Germans we will kill. The more Germans we kill, the fewer of our men will be killed.

Pushing means fewer casualties. I want you all to remember that.

There is one great thing that you men will all be able to say after this war is over and you are home once again. You may be thankful that twenty years from now when you are sitting by the fireplace with your grandson on your knee and he asks you what you did in the great World War II, you WON'T have to cough, shift him to the other knee and say, "Well, your

Granddaddy shoveled shit in Louisiana." No, Sir, you can look him straight in the eye and say, "Son, your Granddaddy rode with the Great Third Army and a Son-of-a-Goddamned-Bitch named Georgie Patton!" That is all.

SIMON VAN BOOY

Friedrich Wilhelm Nietzsche was born in 1844, and is famous for saying that "God is Dead," which many people believe referred to the developing scientific ideas and the secularization of Europe. Although by the age of twenty-four, Nietzsche was appointed to the Chair of Classical Philology at the University of Basel, he resigned his university post in 1879 due to deteriorating health. For the next ten years, he simply wandered around writing important philosophical works. When he was thirty-seven, Nietzsche even fell in love with a twenty-one-year-old Russian aristocrat, though his affection was not returned.

In 1889, Nietzsche suffered a terrible mental breakdown in Turin after watching a horse get beaten savagely by a coachman. Nietzsche never fully recovered his sanity, and died eleven years later in 1900.

Friedrich Nietzche

from *Beyond Good and Evil*

Madness is something rare in individuals—but in groups, parties, peoples, ages, it is the rule.

He who fights with monsters should look to it that he himself does not become a monster. And when you gaze long into an abyss the abyss also gazes into you.

SIMON VAN BOOY

Pieter Bruegel the Elder (born around 1525) was a Netherlandish Renaissance painter. He depicted life as it was for normal people living in the country at the time. Some of his paintings feature biblical or mythical scenes, while others, like *Harvesters*, show peasants lunching on a hillside going about their everyday lives. Bruegel's two sons also became painters.

The Massacre of the Innocents is based on the New Testament story of how King Herod ordered his soldiers to kill all boys aged two and under in and around Bethlehem. By setting the work in a village of his own time, Bruegel may have been suggesting that the stories of the Bible are contemporary, and that events like those so graphically depicted in his painting continue to take place.

Pieter Bruegel the Elder, *The Massacre of the Innocents,*
1565–67

Violence is the last refuge of the incompetent.

—*Isaac Asimov from* Foundation

Born in 1593, Artemisia Gentileschi was one of the first female painters to explore history and religion. She learned to paint in the studio of her father, who was heavily influenced by Caravaggio. Her paintings were unlike her father's in that her style was naturalistic, rather than idealistic. Unable to gain admittance into the academies when she was nineteen, her father had her tutored privately. She is rumored to have died in a plague that swept Naples in 1656.

Judith Beheading Holofernes is from the biblical story of the Hebrew widow Judith who entered the enemy camp of an attacking force, seduced the cruel general named Holofernes, then decapitated him in his drunkenness, thus saving her city. Despite any intentions the artist may have had when creating the piece, it is largely viewed as a painting that depicts heroism in the face of oppression. In this painting, Judith fights to save her home from the forces of tyranny.

Artemisia Gentileschi, *Judith Beheading Holofernes,* 1620

I am not afraid . . . I was born to do this.

—*Joan of Arc*

Men must be either pampered or crushed, because they can get revenge for small injuries, but not for grievous ones.

—*Nicolò Machiavelli*

The Agricola, written by Cornelius Tacitus about two thousand years ago, is about the life of his father-in-law, Julius Agricola—the most well-known governor of Roman Britain. Tacitus, who was a historian of the Roman Empire, writes about Agricola in what is considered a more creative biographical context than a historical one.

In the opening paragraph, Tacitus writes about how Agricola coped with the death of his infant son. Further along, Tacitus writes the speech a British leader is reported to have given—as thirty thousand of his men readied for battle.

Cornelius Tacitus

from *The Agricola*

29. In the beginning of the next summer, Agricola received a severe domestic wound in the loss of a son, about a year old. He bore this calamity, not with the ostentatious firmness which many have affected, nor yet with the tears and lamentations of feminine sorrow; and war was one of the remedies of his grief. Having sent forwards his fleet to spread its ravages through various parts of the coast, in order to excite an extensive and dubious alarm, he marched with an army equipped for expedition, to which he had joined the bravest of the Britons whose fidelity had been approved by a long allegiance, and arrived at the Grampian hills, where the enemy was already encamped. For the Britons, undismayed by the event of the former action, expecting revenge or slavery, and at length taught that the common danger was to be repelled by union alone, had assembled the strength of all their tribes by embassies and confederacies. Upwards of thirty thousand men in arms were now descried; and the youth, together with those of a hale and vigorous age, renowned in war, and bearing their several honorary decorations, were still flocking in; when Calgacus, the most distinguished for birth and valor among the chieftans, is said to have harangued the multitude, gathering round, and eager for battle, after the following manner:

30. "When I reflect on the causes of the war, and the circumstances of our situation, I feel a strong persuasion that our united efforts on the present day will prove the beginning of universal liberty to Britain. For we are all undebased by slavery; and there is no land behind us, nor does even the sea afford a refuge, whilst the Roman fleet hovers around. Thus the use of arms, which is at all times honorable to the brave, now offers the only safety even to cowards. In all the battles which have yet been fought, with various success, against the Romans, our countrymen may be deemed to have reposed their final hopes and resources in us: for we, the noblest sons of Britain, and therefore stationed in its last recesses, far from the view of servile shores, have preserved even our eyes unpolluted by the contact of subjection. We, at the furthest limits both of land and liberty, have been defended to this day by the remoteness of our situation and of our fame. The extremity of Britain is now disclosed; and whatever is unknown becomes an object of magnitude. But there is no nation beyond us; nothing but waves and rocks, and the still more hostile Romans, whose arrogance we cannot escape by obsequiousness and submission. These plunderers of the world, after exhausting the land by their devastations, are rifling the ocean: stimulated by avarice, if their enemy be rich; by ambition, if poor; unsatiated by the East and by the West: the only people who behold wealth

and indigence with equal avidity. To ravage, to slaughter, to usurp under false titles, they call empire; and where they make a desert, they call it peace.

31. "Our children and relations are by the appointment of nature the dearest of all things to us. These are torn away by levies to serve in foreign lands. Our wives and sisters, though they should escape the violation of hostile force, are polluted under names of friendship and hospitality. Our estates and possessions are consumed in tributes; our grain in contributions. Even our bodies are worn down amidst stripes and insults in clearing woods and draining marshes. Wretches born to slavery are once bought, and afterwards maintained by their masters: Britain every day buys, every day feeds, her own servitude. And as among domestic slaves every new comer serves for the scorn and derision of his fellows; so, in this ancient household of the world, we, as the newest and vilest, are sought out to destruction. For we have neither cultivated lands, nor mines, nor harbors, which can induce them to preserve us for our labors. The valor too and unsubmitting spirit of subjects only render them more obnoxious to their masters; while remoteness and secrecy of situation itself, in proportion as it conduces to security, tends to inspire suspicion. Since then all Lopes of mercy are vain, at length assume courage, both you to whom safety and you to whom glory is dear. The Trinobantes, even under a female leader, had force enough to

burn a colony, to storm camps, and, if success had not damped their vigor, would have been able entirely to throw off the yoke; and shall not we, untouched, unsubdued, and struggling not for the acquisition but the security of liberty, show at the very first onset what men Caledonia has reserved for her defence?

32. "Can you imagine that the Romans are as brave in war as they are licentious in peace? Acquiring renown from our discords and dissensions, they convert the faults of their enemies to the glory of their own army; an army compounded of the most different nations, which success alone has kept together, and which misfortune will as certainly dissipate. Unless, indeed, you can suppose that Gauls, and Germans, and (I blush to say it) even Britons, who, though they expend their blood to establish a foreign dominion, have been longer its foes than its subjects, will be retained by loyalty and affection! Terror and dread alone are the weak bonds of attachment; which once broken, they who cease to fear will begin to hate. Every incitement to victory is on our side. The Romans have no wives to animate them; no parents to upbraid their flight. Most of them have either no home, or a distant one. Few in number, ignorant of the country, looking around in silent horror at woods, seas, and a heaven itself unknown to them, they are delivered by the gods, as it were imprisoned and bound, into our hands. Be not terrified with an idle show,

and the glitter of silver and gold, which can neither protect nor wound. In the very ranks of the enemy we shall find our own bands. The Britons will acknowledge their own cause. The Gauls will recollect their former liberty. The rest of the Germans will desert them, as the Usipii have lately done. Nor is there anything formidable behind them: ungarrisoned forts; colonies of old men; municipal towns distempered and distracted between unjust masters and ill-obeying subjects. Here is a general; here an army. There, tributes, mines, and all the train of punishments inflicted on slaves; which whether to bear eternally, or instantly to revenge, this field must determine. March then to battle, and think of your ancestors and your posterity."

33. They received this harangue with alacrity, and testified their applause after the barbarian manner, with songs, and yells, and dissonant shouts. And now the several divisions were in motion, the glittering of arms was beheld, while the most daring and impetuous were hurrying to the front, and the line of battle was forming; when Agricola, although his soldiers were in high spirits, and scarcely to be kept within their intrenchments, kindled additional ardor by these words:

"It is now the eighth year, my fellow-soldiers, in which, under the high auspices of the Roman empire, by your valor and perseverance you have been conquering Britain. In so many expeditions, in so many battles, whether you have been required to exert your courage against the enemy, or your patient labors against the very nature of the country, neither have I ever been dissatisfied with my soldiers, nor you with your general. In this mutual confidence, we have proceeded beyond the limits of former commanders and former armies; and are now become acquainted with the extremity of the island, not by uncertain rumor, but by actual possession with our arms and encampments. Britain is discovered and subdued. How often on a march, when embarrassed with mountains, bogs and rivers, have I heard the bravest among you exclaim, "When shall we descry the enemy? When shall we be led to the field of battle?" At length they are unharbored from their retreats; your wishes and your valor have now free scope; and every circumstance is equally propitious to the victor, and ruinous to the vanquished. For, the greater our glory in having marched over vast tracts of land, penetrated forests, and crossed arms of the sea, while advancing towards the foe, the greater will be our danger and difficulty if we should attempt a retreat. We are inferior to our enemies in knowledge of the country, and less able to command supplies of provision; but we have arms in our hands, and in these we have everything. For myself, it has long been my principle, that a retiring general or army is never safe. Not only, then, are we to reflect that death with honor is preferable to life with ignominy, but to remember that security and glory are seated in the same place. Even to fall in this extremest verge of earth and of nature cannot be thought an inglorious fate.

34. "If unknown nations or untried troops were drawn up against you, I would exhort you from the example of other armies. At present, recollect your own honors, question your own eyes. These are they, who, the last year, attacking by surprise a single legion in the obscurity of the night, were put to flight by a shout: the greatest fugitives of all the Britons, and therefore the longest survivors. As in penetrating woods and thickets the fiercest animals boldly rush on the hunters, while the weak and timorous fly at their very noise; so the bravest of the Britons have long since fallen: the remaining number consists solely of the cowardly and spiritless; whom you see at length within your reach, not because they have stood their ground, but because they are overtaken. Torpid with fear, their bodies are fixed and chained down in yonder field, which to you will speedily be the scene of a glorious and memorable victory. Here bring your toils and services to a conclusion; close a struggle of fifty years with one great day; and convince your country-men, that to the army ought not to be imputed either the protraction of war, or the causes of rebellion."

35. Whilst Agricola was yet speaking, the ardor of the soldiers declared itself; and as soon as he had finished, they burst forth into cheerful acclamations, and instantly flew to arms.

Thus eager and impetuous, he formed them so that the centre was occupied by the auxiliary infantry, in number eight thousand, and three thousand horse were spread in the wings. The legions were stationed in the rear, before the intrenchments; a disposition which would render the victory signally glorious, if it were obtained without the expense of Roman blood; and would ensure support if the rest of the army were repulsed. The British troops, for the greater display of their numbers, and more formidable appearance, were ranged upon the rising grounds, so that the first line stood upon the plain, the rest, as if linked together, rose above one another upon the ascent. The charioteers and horsemen filled the middle of the field with their tumult and careering. Then Agricola, fearing from the superior number of the enemy lest he should be obliged to fight as well on his flanks as in front, extended his ranks; and although this rendered his line of battle less firm, and several of his officers advised him to bring up the legions, yet, filled with hope, and resolute in danger, he dismissed his horse and took his station on foot before the colors.

36. At first the action was carried on at a distance. The Britons, armed with long swords and short targets, with steadiness and dexterity avoided or struck down our missile weapons, and at the same time poured in a torrent of their own. Agricola then encouraged three Batavian and two Tungrian cohorts to fall in and come to close quarters; a method

of fighting familiar to these veteran soldiers, but embarrassing to the enemy from the nature of their armor; for the enormous British swords, blunt at the point, are unfit for close grappling, and engaging in a confined space. When the Batavians, therefore, began to redouble their blows, to strike with the bosses of their shields, and mangle the faces of the enemy; and, bearing down all those who resisted them on the plain, were advancing their lines up the ascent; the other cohorts, fired with ardor and emulation, joined in the charge, and overthrew all who came in their way: and so great was their impetuosity in the pursuit of victory, that they left many of their foes half dead or unhurt behind them. In the meantime the troops of cavalry took to flight, and the armed chariots mingled in the engagement of the infantry; but although their first shock occasioned some consternation, they were soon entangled among the close ranks of the cohorts, and the inequalities of the ground. Not the least appearance was left of an engagement of cavalry; since the men, long keeping their ground with difficulty, were forced along with the bodies of the horses; and frequently, straggling chariots, and affrighted horses without their riders, flying variously as terror impelled them, rushed obliquely athwart or directly through the lines.

37. Those of the Britons who, yet disengaged from the fight, sat on the summits of the hills, and looked with careless contempt on the smallness of our numbers, now began

gradually to descend; and would have fallen on the rear of the conquering troops, had not Agricola, apprehending this very event, opposed four reserved squadron of horse to their attack, which, the more furiously they had advanced, drove them back with the greater celerity. Their project was thus turned against themselves; and the squadrons were ordered to wheel from the front of the battle and fall upon the enemy's rear. A striking and hideous spectacle now appeared on the plain: some pursuing; some striking: some making prisoners, whom they slaughtered as others came in their way. Now, as their several dispositions prompted, crowds of armed Britons fled before inferior numbers, or a few, even unarmed, rushed upon their foes, and offered themselves to a voluntary death. Arms, and carcasses, and mangled limbs, were promiscuously strewed, and the field was dyed in blood. Even among the vanquished were seen instances of rage and valor. When the fugitives approached the woods, they collected, and surrounded the foremost of the pursuers, advancing incautiously, and unacquainted with the country; and had not Agricola, who was everywhere present, caused some strong and lightly-equipped cohorts to encompass the ground, while part of the cavalry dismounted made way through the thickets, and part on horseback scoured the open woods, some disaster would have proceeded from the excess of confidence. But when the enemy saw their pursuers again formed in compact order,

SIMON VAN BOOY

they renewed their flight, not in bodies as before, or waiting for their companions, but scattered and mutually avoiding each other; and thus took their way to the most distant and devious retreats. Night and satiety of slaughter put an end to the pursuit. Of the enemy ten thousand were slain: on our part three hundred and sixty fell; among whom was Aulus Atticus, the praefect of a cohort, who, by his juvenile ardor, and the fire of his horse, was borne into the midst of the enemy.

38. Success and plunder contributed to render the night joyful to the victors; whilst the Britons, wandering and forlorn, amid the promiscuous lamentations of men and women, were dragging along the wounded; calling out to the unhurt; abandoning their habitations, and in the rage of despair setting them on fire; choosing places of concealment, and then deserting them; consulting together, and then separating. Sometimes, on beholding the dear pledges of kindred and affection, they were melted into tenderness, or more frequently roused into fury; insomuch that several, according to authentic information, instigated by a savage compassion, laid violent hands upon their own wives and children. On the succeeding day, a vast silence all around, desolate hills, the distant smoke of burning houses, and not a living soul descried by the scouts, displayed more amply the face of victory. After parties had been detached to all quarters without discovering any certain tracks of the enemy's flight, or any bodies of

them still in arms, as the lateness of the season rendered it impracticable to spread the war through the country, Agricola led his army to the confines of the Horesti. Having received hostages from this people, he ordered the commander of the fleet to sail round the island; for which expedition he was furnished with sufficient force, and preceded by the terror of the Roman name. Pie himself then led back the cavalry and infantry, marching slowly, that he might impress a deeper awe on the newly conquered nations; and at length distributed his troops into their winter-quarters. The fleet, about the same time, with prosperous gales and renown, entered the Trutulensian harbor, whence, coasting all the hither shore of Britain, it returned entire to its former station.

Unknown, An army on the move with its baggage train, 1480

Blood will have blood.

—William Shakespeare from Macbeth

You must be the change you want to see in the world.

—*Mahatma Gandhi*

ACKNOWLEDGMENTS

Amy Baker; Joshua Bodwell; Dr. and Mrs. J. E. Booy; Dr. and Mrs. Raha Booy; Theodore Bouloukos; Douglas and Anita Borroughs, esq.; Milan Bozic; Ken Browar; Bobby Brinson; David Bruson; Dr. S. A. Burgess, academic director and professor at Mediterranean Center for Arts and Sciences; Gabriel Byrne; Tricia Callahan; Michael Colford; Boston Public Library; Christine Corday; Ken and Joann Davis; Justin Dodd; Writing Program at University College Falmouth; Patricio Ferrari; Peggy Flaum; Dr. Giovanni Frazzetto; Colin Gee; Kayleigh George; East Hampton Library; Werner Herzog; Jen Hart; Gregory Henry; Lucas Hunt; Dr. Mickey Kempner;

Alan Kleinberg; Hilary Knight; Bryan LeBoeuf; Eva Lontscharitsch; Alain Malraux; Lisa Mamo; Metropolitan Museum of Art; Metropolitan Opera; MoMA; Dr. Edmund Miller; Cal Morgan; National Gallery, London: Dr. William Neal; New York Society Library; New York School of Visual Arts; Lukas Ortiz; Rogers Memorial Library of Southampton; Jonathan Rabinowitz; Alberto Rojas; Ivan Shaw; Hala Schlub; Philip G. Spitzer; Virginia Stanley; Dolores Henry; the Connolly family; the Gaddis family; the O'Brien family; McNally-Jackson Booksellers; Prairie Lights Books; Shakespeare & Co. Paris; Andy Spade; Anthony Sperdutti; Fred Volkmer; Amy Vreeland; Wim Wenders; Dr. Barbara Wersba; Phaedra Athanasiou at the Brooklyn Academy of Music; and Les Arts Florissants, under the musical direction of William Christie.

I would like to express an even greater debt of gratitude to the following two people:

Carrie Kania, for her brilliance, her vision, her love of Samuel Beckett and Henry Miller, and her unrivaled sense of personal style and her collection of Vivienne Westwood shoes.

My deepest thanks go to Michael Signorelli for his sparkling intelligence, superhuman attention to detail, old-world courtesy, and the fact that he's a fly-fisherman.

PERMISSIONS

Every effort has been made to trace the ownership of copyrighted material and to make full acknowledgment of its use. The editor regrets any errors or omissions, which will be corrected in subsequent editions upon notification in writing to the publisher.